GOD BEYOND KNOWLEDGE

LIBRARY OF PHILOSOPHY AND RELIGION

General Editor: John Hick, H. G. Wood
Professor of Theology, University of Birmingham

This new series of books will explore contemporary religious understandings of man and the universe. The books will be contributions to various aspects of the continuing dialogues between religion and philosophy, between scepticism and faith, and between the different religions and ideologies. The authors will represent a correspondingly wide range of viewpoints. Some of the books in the series will be written for the general educated public and others for a more specialised philosophical or theological readership.

Already published

William H. Austin	THE RELEVANCE OF NATURAL SCIENCE TO THEOLOGY
Paul Badham	CHRISTIAN BELIEFS ABOUT LIFE AFTER DEATH
Patrick Burke	THE FRAGILE UNIVERSE
William Lane Craig	THE *KALĀM* COSMOLOGICAL ARGUMENT
Lynn A. de Silva	THE PROBLEM OF THE SELF IN BUDDHISM AND CHRISTIANITY
Padmasiri de Silva	AN INTRODUCTION TO BUDDHIST PSYCHOLOGY
Ramchandra Gandhi	THE AVAILABILITY OF RELIGIOUS IDEAS
J. C. A. Gaskin	HUME'S PHILOSOPHY OF RELIGION
H. A. Hodges	GOD BEYOND KNOWLEDGE
Hywel D. Lewis	PERSONS AND LIFE AFTER DEATH
Hugo A. Meynell	AN INTRODUCTION TO THE PHILOSOPHY OF BERNARD LONERGAN
F. C. T. Moore	THE PSYCHOLOGICAL BASIS OF MORALITY
Dennis Nineham	THE USE AND ABUSE OF THE BIBLE
Bernard M. G. Reardon	HEGEL'S PHILOSOPHY OF RELIGION
John J. Shepherd	EXPERIENCE, INFERENCE AND GOD
Patrick Sherry	RELIGION, TRUTH AND LANGUAGE-GAMES
Robert Young	FREEDOM, RESPONSIBILITY AND GOD

God Beyond Knowledge

H. A. Hodges
Edited by W. D. Hudson

BARNES & NOBLE
BOOKS
10 East 53d St. New York 10022
(a division of Harper & Row Publishers, Inc.)

First published 1979 by
THE MACMILLAN PRESS LTD
London and Basingstoke

Published in the U.S.A. 1979 by
HARPER & ROW PUBLISHERS, INC.
BARNES & NOBLE IMPORT DIVISION

Printed in Great Britain

Library of Congress Cataloging in Publication Data

Hodges, Herbert Arthur, 1905-
  God beyond knowledge.

  (Library of philosophy & religion)
  1. God—Addresses, essays, lectures.   I. Title.
BT102.H63   231   77-22634
ISBN 0-06-492922-1

Contents

H. A. Hodges   vii

Preface   xi

Part I: The Problem of 'God'   1
  1 Natural Theology, Old and New   3
  2 Knowledge, Evidence and 'God'   10
  3 The Elusiveness of Theological Statements   24
  4 Standard and Non-standard Usages of 'God'   37

Part II: 'And heard great argument about it and about'   45
  5 The Genesis of 'God'   47
  6 Metaphysical Arguments for the Existence of God   60
  7 Meaningfulness and Mystery   75
  8 Not Proven   91

Part III: Religious Experience and Faith   99
  9 Modes of Experiential Contact with God   101
  10 Being and Beyond Being   112
  11 Shifting Perspectives   124
  12 Faith and Commitment   133

Part IV: Behind Belief and Non-belief   137
  13 *Credo ut fiam*   139
  14 The Divided Mind of *Homo sapiens*   157
  15 Choice, No Choice and Self-Choice   169
  16 Analytical Philosophy and the Believer   175

Index   182

H. A. Hodges (1905–1976)

Herbert Arthur Hodges was born in Sheffield on 4 January 1905 and died in Reading on 2 July 1976. His father was a commercial traveller, occasionally unemployed, and his mother had been an elementary school teacher. He spent his youth in the Yorkshire steel town. Not only was there evidence of this in the traces of a Yorkshire accent which he retained throughout life, but also in his strong and lasting sympathy with the aspirations of the unprivileged for education and a better environment.

Scholarships took him to the King Edward VII School in Sheffield and then to Oxford. He was a classical scholar at Balliol College, taking a first in Honour Moderations in 1924 and a first in Literae Humaniores in 1926. He gained numerous academic awards including the John Locke Scholarship. After a short period as a Lecturer in Philosophy at New College, Oxford, he became in 1928 a Lecturer at Reading University. In 1932 he took the Oxford Doctor of Philosophy degree for work on Wilhelm Dilthey and then, in 1934, became Professor of Philosophy at Reading. He occupied his chair at Reading for thirty-five years, declining invitations to return to Oxford because he found life in the expanding redbrick university so congenial.

Among his Oxford teachers the one who probably exerted the strongest influence upon him was A. D. Lindsay, from whom he derived his interest in Dilthey. Hodges became friendly at Oxford with Austen Farrer and this relationship deeply influenced his religious, as well as his intellectual, development. In 1939 he married one of his pupils, Vera Joan Willis, who bore him two sons and a daughter.

Until his late years at least, Professor Hodges saw himself primarily as a teacher, rather than a writer, of philosophy. It was his practice to lecture from very brief notes but this did not indicate any lack of careful preparation. Throughout his long teaching career he read widely and thought strenuously in order to ensure that his lectures would be as clear and informative as he could make them.

Besides classical Greek and Latin, he read French, German and
Italian with ease. His interest in the Bible induced him to teach
himself Hebrew. He became fascinated by the Welsh and this led
him to learn their language and study their literature.

As Professor Hodges' philosophical interests widened, so did his
audiences. He began to think about political philosophy, aesthetics,
the philosophy of science and religion. He was often in demand for
courses organised by the Workers' Educational Association, and
frequently invited to lecture at the Services Colleges on subjects
such as Marxism. In 1949, he publicly debated the credibility of
religious belief with an atheistic colleague from Reading University
in six half-hour broadcasts on the B.B.C. Home Service, entitled
'Clearing the Ground'. The numerous Christian organisations with
which he came to be associated regularly called upon him to address
them on the various philosophical questions which arise in connection with religious belief.

Although he saw his main work as that of a lecturer, Professor
Hodges did in fact write extensively, particularly in the later part of
his career. His early work on Dilthey found expression in two books,
Wilhelm Dilthey: An Introduction (1944) and *The Philosophy of Wilhelm
Dilthey* (1952). The fruit of his long reflections on religious belief is
contained in the Riddell Lectures, delivered in the University of
Durham and entitled *Languages, Standpoints and Attitudes* (1953); and
in the Gifford Lectures, given before the University of Aberdeen in
1956 and 1957, the substance of which is to be found in this volume.
A more personal account of how he reconciled philosophical
scepticism and religious belief is contained in a small book, which
awaits publication and which he entitled *The Mind's Road to God*.
Professor Hodges was a lay theologian as well as a professional
philosopher and in this capacity he published *Christianity and the
Modern World View* (1949), *Patterns of Atonement* (1955) and *Death and
Life have Contended* (1964), all of which were highly thought of by his
fellow believers. He also wrote, with others, two books about hymns.
A Rapture of Praise (with A. M. Allchin, 1966) is an appraisal of the
hymns of John and Charles Wesley; and *A Homage to Ann Griffiths*
(1976) contains Hodges' translations of many of her Welsh hymns.
His interest in the Oecumenical Movement is evident in *Anglicanism
and Orthodoxy* (1955). In addition to these books, he published
numerous papers throughout his life on the philosophy of politics, of
art, of education, of religion, etc.

Indifferent health troubled him for many years and this prevented him from living as active a life as, no doubt, he would have wished. Nevertheless, his sympathies and interests extended far beyond the narrow confines of the academic scene. In his leisure he delighted in what he liked to call exploring England. Having spent his boyhood in an industrial environment, he deplored his own ignorance of the countryside and systematically tried to inform it. During the war he learned to ride a bicycle and explored the unsignposted lanes and roads within a ten-mile radius of the town, meticulously marking them off in pencil on a road atlas as he got to know them. He later widened the radius to fifty miles on buying a car. Among his books there is a solid little volume on the wild flowers of Britain and, in the margins, he has noted in his neat handwriting the date and place of his first knowing encounter with each species. Eventually he became something of an authority on the topography and local history of Berkshire. Music and art gave him great pleasure throughout his life and these interests, combined with his interest in Socialism, made him from 1954 to 1973 an enthusiastic Master of the Guild of St George, which exists to express and promote the ideas of John Ruskin. When he was made a member of a Royal Commission, set up to investigate Betting, Lotteries and Gaming, he took his duties very seriously and spent a lot of time between 1949 and 1951 visiting the, to him, strange world of racecourses and gaming tables in order to discover for himself precisely what went on there.

Professor Hodges' most cherished relationships and concerns, however, were those of a Churchman. He gives an account of his churchly pilgrimage in his contribution to *They Became Anglicans* (edited by Dewi Morgan, London, 1959). Having been brought up within the Methodist Church, he functioned, during his first undergraduate year, as one of its lay preachers in the villages around Oxford. By the beginning of his third year, however, he had completely lost his Christian beliefs and professed himself an atheist. It was his comprehensive philosophical scepticism about the possibility of knowledge of any kind, scientific as well as religious, which undermined his faith; and in telling us this, he remarks that the question, 'How can critical thinking be effective as criticism without becoming destructive of thought and life?', was, in fact, with him throughout his life from the age of fifteen. Nevertheless, when he was twenty-three he returned to the Christian fold as a member of the Church of England. His conversion was not so much to Anglicanism as to Catholicism, in the sense in which Roman

Catholics, all Orthodox people and some Anglicans can be described as Catholics. Of these options, he chose to become an Anglican because he felt that within the Church of England he could participate in the fullness of the Catholic tradition whilst enjoying the greatest freedom to enquire into all aspects of the Christian faith.

Professor Hodges was a most enthusiastic supporter of the Oecumenical Movement. He suggests that, strange as it may seem, it was only after becoming an Anglo-Catholic that he gained a deep appreciation of the Free Church tradition in general and of Methodism in particular; and he tells us that he found contact with the doctrine and worship of the Orthodox Church a transforming experience, which helped him to see what was essential in Catholicism and what was not. He represented the Church of England at World Council of Churches Conferences in Amsterdam and Montreal; and he was a member of the Archbishops' Commission on Intercommunion, helping to frame the Report which it presented in 1968. His conviction that the Churches must move towards reunion was sincerely held and he readily responded to any invitations to help work out the doctrinal bases upon which closer church relations could be built. He was deeply disappointed when the Anglican–Methodist Conversations failed to bring those two communions together.

Professor Hodges was a shy man and some people found him taciturn and elusive. He occasionally said – inaccurately – to colleagues that he had no small talk. Within his family and by close friends, however, he is spoken of as a most devoted individual and those who worked alongside him in the academic world remember him as a courteous and considerate colleague. He enjoyed the company of non-academic people and used to refer to the pleasure he had derived during the war from serving with men from all walks of life in the Home Guard. Archbishop Anthony Bloom no doubt spoke for many of his Christian friends when, upon hearing the news of his death, he wrote to Mrs Hodges: 'He was to us "a Light burning and shining" – bright with a purity and a lucidity I have never met before or after, warm with a shy, chaste warmth, that of worship and devotion. He is now within the Eternal Light which shone so clearly and so gently through him . . .'

W.D.H.

Preface

These chapters are a much revised version of the Gifford Lectures which I delivered at Aberdeen in 1956–57 under the title *The Logic of Religious Thinking*. There were twenty-one lectures, and the substance of them, brought up to date, is now presented in sixteen chapters. Though no part of the original text survives, the matters dealt with, the contentions advanced, and the overall arrangement of the argument, are the same.

In offering these thoughts to a wider public, I look back with gratitude to the University of Aberdeen for providing the initial stimulus, and for the friendly way in which my lectures there were received.

A word about my theme and my approach to it. My theme is man's belief in God – not the theoretical entity constructed by philosophers to round off their systems, but the God of the great theist religions, the God in whom men believe, whom they worship and serve and love and to union with whom they aspire. And though I am familiar with the Christian tradition, I do not write in support or defence of that tradition. I seek to penetrate to what underlies all the religious traditions and makes them possible, namely the readiness of man to acknowledge Something above and beyond and around and within himself, on which he is utterly dependent and yet with which he can enter into a kind of reciprocity. The tendency to such an acknowledgment is obviously deep-seated in the human soul, though it is often held in check by counter-tendencies. Where the acknowledgment is made, it is usually amplified on the lines of one or other of the religious systems, but that is no part of my subject. 'God', the extreme complexity and inherent dialectic of the concept, the unremitting attempts of men to rationalise it and their perpetual failure, and the resulting conflicts in individual minds and in human culture at large – that is my theme.

I could not attempt to draw up a list of those to whom I am indebted. My literary sources will be obvious to any reader who has known the same sources. Equally important has been the constant contact, over many years, with people who in their various ways shared something of my concern, and whose sympathetic interest encouraged me to keep on at this somewhat complex task. The deficiencies in my accomplishment of it are of course to be set down to my own account.

Part I
THE PROBLEM OF 'GOD'

1 Natural Theology, Old and New

The terms of the Gifford foundation leave the lecturers free as to the manner in which they deal with their subject, but the subject itself is clearly defined. It is to be natural theology. This is a term with a recognised meaning, and I intend to keep as close as I can to what the term signifies. It signifies a discussion of the existence and attributes of God, carried on by the exercise of human reason in application to the facts of common experience, but without appeal to authority in the shape of any revelation alleged to have been made by God to men. It is thus clearly distinguished from revealed theology, which is what most people understand by the world 'theology' today. Revealed theology either begins by assuming that a divine revelation exists, or makes it its first business to persuade the reader that it exists. It then explores the content of this revelation, setting it forth clearly and systematically and drawing out all the consequences which can be shown to follow from it. Revealed theology is the intellectual side of a revealed religion. Natural theology on the other hand is an exercise in free thinking. In real life, indeed, the natural theologian may be a believer in some revealed religion, but his business as a natural theologian is to set that belief aside and try how far he can get without it. For such a thinker, natural theology must be a sustained exercise in irony. He must continually say less than he believes, in order not to say more than he thinks he can prove.

Natural theology so conceived has a long tradition behind it, reaching back in Europe two thousand years and more; and always it has been philosophical theology, a kind of work done by philosophers. But it has not been the only kind of work that they did. It belongs to that branch of their work which is called metaphysics.

Metaphysics (according to the classic concept) looks more widely and sees more deeply than any other enquiry pursued by natural reason. It presupposes the common sensory experience of mankind and the body of knowledge and belief, based upon this, which we nowadays call common sense. It presupposes also the special sciences, such as physics, astronomy or biology, which by skilled investigation bring about a great increase of our knowledge in particular fields. Metaphysics presupposes all this, but goes beyond it. As distinct from common sense, which deals with things as observed and experienced, it tries to get to the bottom of things, to find their innermost structure; and in contrast with the special sciences, each of which has a limited field, it tries to deal with the totality of things.

To get to the bottom of things and at the same time to see them comprehensively is a vast and bold enterprise; yet there is more. Besides being a survey of all that is, metaphysics is also a synthesis of existence and value. This too was one of its aims from the beginning: to find a unity between the kind of thing we say when we discuss existing things and the kind of thing we say when we make judgments of value or lay down rules of conduct. It came to be thought that 'good' could be understood in such a way that goodness was seen to be one of the fundamental and inalienable attributes of being; so that the doctrine of being included in itself the doctrine of good, and the supreme source of being, if there was one, must at the same time be the supreme source of goodness.

This being the task which metaphysics set itself, natural theology came in as the fulfilment of the task. From his analysis of the nature of all that is, the metaphysician concluded that the natural world in which we find ourselves cannot possibly be the whole of what exists. It is able to exist, and to be what it is, only because it is derived from, and dependent upon, a source of being which can be shown to be independent of space and time, of matter, change and contingency, and to be in some sense intelligent. Furthermore, since being entails goodness, the source of being must be also the source of good, itself (or rather, himself) good above all goods, and in some sense the last end of all our striving. This sounds very like what the great religions, such as Christianity or Judaism or Islam, say about God; but the claim is that it is reached as the result of honest reasoning from the metaphysician's own proper premises.

It should be added that not all metaphysical reasoning has followed this road. Some philosophers have conceived the supreme source of things on different lines from standard theism, and some have failed to find a supreme source of any kind at all. There have been materialists. There have been positivists. And so natural theology cannot be described simply as the ultimate outcome of the metaphysical quest. It is no more than one line of thought which has been popular with metaphysicians at certain times and places; though the length of time during which it flourished, and the rich development of which it proved to be capable, must in any case command our respect.

The conception of natural theology which we have been examining is part of a way of thought in which philosophy was expected to provide knowledge about the nature of things, and to see more deeply into it than either common observation or empirical research could do; in which philosophers were ready to tell us what the universe is like and how it comes to be like this. It would not be true to say that there are no philosophers now who write in this time-honoured fashion. Even the twentieth century has seen several who could be described as word-painters of the universe. Nevertheless the prevailing style of philosophy nowadays is different from this. For an account of what the world is like we now look not to metaphysics but to natural science, and what cannot be found out by scientific methods we tend to believe cannot be found out at all. If it can still be said that there is a world which philosophy explores, it is not the world of being, but the world of human discourse. That is to say, we ask not what things really are and whence they come, but how we come to know them, what part is played in this on the one hand by sense-experience and on the other hand by linguistic symbols, how knowledge is gained or opinion formed, how attitude are taken up and judgments made. Instead of asking what is the relation between the real and the good, we ask what is the relation, if there is one at all, between what we do when we explore the world of existing things and what we do when we make judgments of value and take up moral or aesthetic attitudes. Where God is concerned we ask not whether he exists or what he is like, but how people come to say he exists, how we should understand what they say about him, what is meant by 'believing in' him, and what could be a valid reason for or against believing. In a word, natural theology nowadays is not so much about God as about 'God'.

It is in this modern spirit that I myself approach the question. Not God but 'God' is my subject in what follows.

So far this distinctively modern style in philosophy has been more fully developed in English-speaking countries than elsewhere. Nevertheless I do not believe that this is a local or national peculiarity (though the past history of English philosophy does provide a congenial background for it) or that it is a fashion which will pass. I agree with those who from time to time in the last forty years have spoken of a revolution taking place in philosophy. A revolution means a fundamental change in aims and methods, and that is what has occurred. It has always been characteristic of philosophy to concern itself with ultimates – ultimate realities, ultimate principles, ultimate questions – and we have now acquired a new conception of what the ultimate questions for the human intelligence actually are: not about the ultimate stuff of reality or the causes of the universe, nor about ultimate principles from which all human knowledge can be shown to flow, but questions about the uses and functions of language. Organised human thought is impossible without language, and the different departments of thought, such as mathematics, empirical science, value-judgments and imaginative creations, may be regarded as so many different games which we play with language. Each has its own worthwhileness and its own rules of play, and it is today a major concern for us to sort out the different games, analyse the special character of each, and guard against confusion between one game and another.

It is my personal belief that beyond these questions about the uses of language lie yet more difficult questions, of a kind sometimes known nowadays as existential questions. The way in which these questions have been handled abroad has not so far found much favour in the English-speaking countries where linguistic interests and analytical methods hold sway. I think the existential questions are in the end unavoidable, but the time for a concerted exploration of them has not yet come, nor will it come until the work of analysis has been carried further than it has been hitherto.

The dominating factor in the intellectual world in the last hundred years has been natural science. All sections of society have felt its influence both in their ways of life and in their thinking, and in philosophy the revolution would hardly have been possible without it. It is not primarily a matter of the new picture of the universe which results from the scientist's explorations, though it would be hard for any department of human thinking to be uninfluenced by that. But essentially it is a matter of discovering a new thought-model, a new way of stating questions and answering them. What kind of mind, what outlook and interests, does a man need to have if he is to be a scientist? What does he take for granted? What does he call in question? How are verbal and other symbols related to experience in his thinking? And what is meant by 'experience' in this connection? What does he allow to count as evidence? How, and under what conditions, does he frame hypotheses which go beyond observed or observable fact?

To answer these questions is to enunciate a new thought-paradigm, a new and more rigorous definition of what is to be counted as knowledge (and so, perhaps, by implication, of what is to be acknowledged as reality). And it raises further questions. Can the scientific method be extended beyond its original home in the investigation of nature, into other realms of human thought and discourse? Apparently not into all. And what, then, of those realms in which it cannot be applied? We shall have to revise our conception of them, to reconsider their claims on our attention, to decide what status and authority they can claim, if they cannot rank as knowledge in the new rigorous definition of that term.

This applies to all discourse about 'God', whether it be philosophical, i.e. metaphysical, on the lines of the old natural theology, or whether it be theological in the sense of moving within the thought-world of a specific religion. All such discourse must be subjected to a logical and semantic analysis. Here is this word 'God' and a whole vocabulary of words and phrases connected with it, and here are large numbers of people who habitually talk in this language. What they say is mostly not verifiable by common observation, nor has it the well-known characteristics of scientific discourse. On the other hand it is hard to dismiss it as having no serious import. It has some kind of logical structure; for its speakers understand one another well enough to be able to discuss and debate and to construct reasoned systems of doctrine. And they clearly are able to connect it in some way with the experience of life, though outsiders notoriously find it hard to understand how they do this. Here then are our terms of reference. We want to know what God-discourse is about, and why some people find it important and convincing, while others find it neither the one nor the other. At what points and in what ways does it connect with experience? What conventions are followed in giving an application to this kind of verbal expression? What is it for a theological assertion to be 'believed'? What counts as evidence in this sphere? What sort of considerations carry weight in an argument? And how is all this related to other organised bodies of discourse, especially to empirical science?

In view of all that has been said, we can hardly limit ourselves to discussing 'God' as the natural theology of the past has presented the concept. That would be mere antiquarianism. We must look more widely at the various ways in which the term is used, and especially in religion, between which and 'God' there is a close connection. There will be more to be said later about what is called 'religion' and about the part played by 'God' in it. Suffice it here to say that there is a standard conception of religion, which treats it as a complex of ideas, sentiments and activities centred upon God, and a standard conception of God, which treats him as an object – the only final and ultimate object – of religious attachment. The religions do not all speak alike; but Christianity and Judaism and Islam form a clearly distinguishable group together. They have strong historical affinities, they have to some extent a comparable spiritual life and doctrine, and in mediaeval times they spoke more or less a common philosophical language. And while Hinduism as a whole is something apart from this group, it too contains elements with which the western group cannot but recognise an affinity.[1] There is thus a classical tradition of theism, exemplified in different ways and in different degrees in the literature of all these religions, which stands out as a possible object of study, and it is this that I shall try to have in mind when I speak of theism.

Theism in this sense is not just a philosophical theory, though its most mature intellectual formulations owe much to philosophical influence. On a broad view we can discern four features of it which will prove to be of interest to us in our further enquiries:

(a) At its heart is a conception of God as the absolute *prius*, wholly unconditioned, the unoriginated origin of all else that is.

(b) This absolute is also conceived as an intelligent being, wise and good, the creator and ruler of the world and in particular of human beings.

(c) It is believed that human beings individually, and according to certain doctrines also collectively, in groups, can enter into relationships with God, of a kind which it is customary to describe in the language of human personal relationships. The precise character of the relationship with God which they claim to have varies according to their own beliefs and attitudes. In many instances they speak of him and to him in the language of personal intimacy, friendship and even love. This is something which rarely emerges in

---

[1] Buddhism is at an even further remove, and cannot rank as a form of theism in the sense in which I am using the word; though even here there are points where comparisons can be made.

a predominantly philosophical system, though some Platonists and some Stoics have approximated to it.

(d) At the same time it is agreed doctrine that God is beyond human understanding. This is not merely the hasty reaction of the ordinary man disheartened at the sight of the problems which arise. It is also the considered judgment of the philosophical theologians, who on grounds of metaphysics and theory of knowledge work out a doctrine of the divine incomprehensibility. (It is not always realised what a strong streak of agnosticism the traditional philosophical theology bears within itself.) And again, when the life of piety develops along the lines which are generally called mystical, it arrives by its own road at an apprehension of God as the ultimate Mystery – an apprehension which, surprisingly, does not at all inhibit the relations of personal intimacy which the contemplative has with his God.

Theism in this standard sense is my subject in the following pages. The analysis of this in logical and epistemological terms, as already described, is natural theology as I conceive it in twentieth-century terms. And while it clearly differs from the traditional natural theology which Lord Gifford had in mind, it stands in direct descent from it. Moreover, it will have to include a serious consideration of the traditional doctrine itself. For in spite of all the recent changes in the philosophical climate, old-style natural theology is not yet dead. There are still people who teach it and who believe it to be a permanent possession of the human mind. Even if that were not so, its prevalence in the past would still be enough to make it something which we could not safely ignore. If we are to make a study of what men think and say about God, old-style natural theology is after all a classic specimen of that. But neither can we ignore the radical questionings which are characteristic of our own time when every tradition is brought under criticism, and discussion becomes increasingly difficult because language itself is no longer a reliable means of communication. These most recent tendencies must also be explored and assessed.

We are, then, still in line with the age-long tradition to which Lord Gifford pointed us; but we are carrying on the line of that tradition into an age and an intellectual situation which he could not have foreseen.

2 Knowledge, Evidence and 'God'

Is the existence of God something which we can claim to know? Or is it merely a belief for which a more or less strong case can be made? Or is it a fantasy for which there is no reasonable case at all?

Our answer to these questions will depend on what we mean by 'knowledge'; and this is a word which has long had, and has now, a variety of usages. It would be a mistake to suppose that there is one clearly identifiable something called 'knowledge', which one either has or has not got. 'Knowledge' is always a success-word, signifying some kind of achievement or attainment. I am not here concerned with knowing in the sense of knowing-how, but of knowing-that or knowing-what, i.e. knowing that such-and-such is the case, or knowing what so-and-so is or is like. And here the word always connotes a well-grounded confidence on the part of the knower. He has, and is aware that he has, a right to the views which he asserts.

KNOWLEDGE AND THE SCIENTIFIC MODEL

Philosophy has always been interested in the nature of knowledge, the difference between knowledge and belief, the range of possible knowledge, and similar questions. There have been many theories of knowledge. One tendency, recurring often in all periods of philosophical history, has been to limit 'knowledge' to those cognitions which exhibit complete logical certitude. One can find this in mathematics and in pure formal logic, but outside these two spheres only in those special cases which are amenable to deductive reasoning. All empirical cognition of contingent fact is incapable of that certitude which constitutes knowledge; it must be classed as 'opinion' and can never rise above probability.

Since the Renaissance the adoption of new methods in natural science, with the astonishing progress to which it has led, has altered the perspective. Of course it is still true that scientific theories, however massively supported by empirical evidence and however impressive in their comprehensiveness and coherence, fall short of logical certitude. It is recognised to be a feature of this kind of enquiry, that in it all achieved results are provisional. But the constantly growing body of results to which scientific enquiry leads is now seen to be in its own way not less impressive than the results achieved in mathematics, all the more so because it is now clear to us that science brings us into touch with real existence and mathematics does not. It is felt to be pedantic to deny to science the name of 'knowledge'; indeed, science has largely taken the place in modern thought which mathematics held among the ancients, as the acknowledged model of what knowledge should be. Modern logic and theory of knowledge are to a considerable extent an analysis of the nature and implications of scientific method.

Not all sciences exhibit the scientific model with equal degrees of perfection. Not all of them merit the term 'exact sciences'. Some have had to wait and struggle for recognition as being sciences at all; that was once true of biology, then of psychology, and today of the social sciences. It is a question of how nearly they can approximate to the exploratory versatility and critical rigour of the exact sciences. Experimental psychology has now perhaps won its place, but what of depth psychology? And psychical research notoriously hovers still in the penumbra of intellectual respectability. And so on.

Of course there is a vast body of thought and experience embracing our every-day awareness of the world around us and of the people in it, which no one would claim as scientific. This body of thought and experience is the common possession of us all. It is essentially empirical, being based on perception and tested in action by trial and error, and it serves as the take-off point from which science, properly so called, sets out upon its exploratory flights; indeed the only difference between it and science lies in the rigour and persistence with which the appeal to experience is carried out. It would be linguistically odd to refuse to call this body of common thought and experience 'knowledge' and insist on calling it opinion. But of course this means that we must recognise a stricter and a looser concept of 'knowledge'.

We need not dwell on the point. It matters nothing to us that there is a sense in which common human beliefs and experiences can be called knowledge; for we are concerned with theology, which has not a secure place among those beliefs and experiences, but is a matter of general debate. The question whether theology can rank as knowledge is really the question whether it can meet the challenge of the logical standards proper to science. We shall find that it cannot.

Some theists, hearing this said, will object that theology should not be judged by these standards, that it is a different kind of reality-discernment from science, though a not less assured and well-grounded one. What kind of reality-discernment then is this? The answer is given by appeal either to the knowledge which human beings have of one another as persons, their understanding of one another's thoughts and experiences and characters, or to an alleged 'higher' or metaphysical mode of knowledge.

As regards our knowledge of other persons, I do not believe the contention can stand. It is empirical knowledge, not different in any essential from our common knowledge of things or indeed from empirical science. It depends on perception, though in a peculiar way of its own. Particular thoughts or feelings or volitions in another mind become accessible to us only as they find expression in word or action, in mien or gesture. They are neither directly presented in perception, like sensible objects, nor inferred as part of a scientific theory, like basic physical particles. They are intuitively read in their expressions. As for our knowledge of a person's character, it is constructed inductively from many particular observations, and the construction is always open to question and to revision, as all inductive constructions must be.

What the objector is thinking of is probably the fact that our knowing of one another is so much bound up with our reciprocal intercourse. We do not stand like detached observers to study our friend's mental processes, we read his thoughts intuitively in the act of conversing with him, in a give-and-take of mutual stimulation and response, all the time treating him as a person, an *alter ego*, and not as an object. Or so they say. But in fact, although the other person is not a *mere* object but one who requires to be treated, and normally is treated, with respect, yet in certain aspects and in certain relationships he *is* an object after all, and when I have dealings with him I am compelled to use my wits, to observe his expressions, to guess his meaning, to test his responses and finally to form a conclusion; all of which is empirical and indeed experimental thinking, whether it is customary to call it scientific or not. If, as these theists maintain, our knowledge of God is obtained in a kind of personal intercourse with him such as we have with one another, then it is after all empirical-experimental knowledge. The really important difference then is that while we can see other people's bodies and check our understanding of them by following their changing utterances and expressions from moment to moment, God has no body for us to see, our interpretation of his thoughts and purposes from the course of observed events is schematic and highly debatable, and his very existence is conjectural in a sense in which the existence of other human minds is not. In a word, assimilating our knowledge of God to our knowledge of other human persons does nothing to strengthen its logical position.

As for theology being a metaphysical kind of cognition, a 'higher knowledge' ranking above empirical knowing, two things may be meant:

(a) It may be meant that there is an intuitive apprehension of the highest realms of being and specifically of God, the highest of all. Such an apprehension seems to be claimed by mystics, and many religions include a tradition of meditation and thought-discipline which is supposed to lead towards it. A less esoteric and more imaginative form of apprehension is found in the God-vision of which I speak below in Chapter 5. This is a regular feature of the religious consciousness, and finds constant expression in the scriptures and devotional literature of the various religions. Both in its more popular imaginative form as the God-vision, and in its more esoteric form as mystical contemplation, this intuitive apprehension of what are taken to be metaphysical realities is unquestionably a real experience, of which more will have to be said later. And it comes to those who have it with a force of conviction which impels them sometimes to speak of it as a kind of knowledge. However, one is not always in the enjoyment of compelling metaphysical intuitions; one returns to live in that whole range of experience which constitutes us as men, and in the activities and aims by which that experience is shaped, and then one sees that the word 'knowledge, embodies ideals of clarity and distinctness which are essential to the humanity of man, but in which the 'higher knowledge' is conspicuously lacking.

(b) Or what is meant may be the traditional 'science' of metaphysics, of which I shall have to speak in Chapters 6, 7 and 8. Suffice it here to say that, as a form of intellectual enquiry distinct from empirical science, I agree with most modern philosophers in finding it lacking in cogency.

In sum, I agree with the prevailing modern view that any

cognitive enterprise deserves to be called knowledge in so far, and only so far, as it approximates to the scientific model. If theology does not meet the requirements of that model, then theology is not to be called knowledge. In this and the following chapter, I shall spell out its failure to qualify as empirical knowledge. Then later I shall examine the customary way of presenting it as metaphysical knowledge, and indicate how that too breaks down.

That theology is not knowledge does not entail that it must be dismissed out of hand as a waste of time; but it means that different questions must be asked about theology. If it is not knowledge, what is it? And, being what it is, should it be recognised as intellectually respectable? To what should we be committing ourselves in giving it such recognition, or on the other hand in refusing to do so? These questions open up the existential dimension to which I alluded briefly in Chapter 1, and with an excursion into which this book will end.

But now to the immediate question, viz. whether theology satisfies the requirements of the scientific model in respect of method and cogency. What are these requirements?

THE REQUIREMENTS OF EMPIRICAL KNOWLEDGE

Modern theory of knowledge on the whole is empiricist. That is to say, it lays down that all knowledge of existing things must come from experience, either by direct observation or by inference, in accordance with scientific method, from what is observed.

The ordinary man responds readily to the claim that experience is our only ultimate source for knowledge of reality. To a practical man, as most men are, it rings true. And in these days of empirical science and empiricist philosophy it is inevitable that theists should claim to base their assertions on experience too. The claim has even been made in due form: theism is analogous to a scientific hypothesis, which is verified by acting on it and obtaining the predicted results. Less formally, very many theists would be disposed to say that their belief finds continual illustration and confirmation in their general experience of life.

I am not speaking here of what is called religious experience. That will come in later in a different context. The phrase covers a wide variety of experience, but a common feature of them all is that, while they play a prominent part in some people's lives, others do not appear to have them, or at any rate cannot recognise them as being the same experiences of which the theists speak. Religious experience is thus not part of that common experience of mankind on which our empirical knowledge and beliefs are founded. It is confined to certain persons, and any evidential value which it may possess is a value only for them and for anyone who is willing to accept their testimony.

The attempt to establish theism by empirical evidence runs into fatal difficulties, as we shall see.

One difficulty springs to mind at once: God, in the standard sense of the term, is not a possible object of experience. Not merely by the accident of our circumstances, but essentially, by his very nature, he is incapable of coming under human observation. If we are to learn anything about such an object from experience, we must learn it indirectly, by inference from other objects which are observable. That in itself need be no insuperable obstacle. The empirical science of physics informs us in great detail about the various kinds of particle which are the smallest units (so far as we yet know) out of which the physical world is built up. These particles are by their very nature imperceptible. We cannot describe their appearance, since they do not appear. But we can describe them in terms of space, time and motion, of mass and electric charge and energy, all of which can be expressed in mathematical language. So we can formulate hypotheses and test them experimentally, and the whole theory constructed in terms of these sub-atomic entities is agreed to be thus massively verified. The case is very different with God. He cannot be described with a remotely comparable degree of precision; nor therefore can the experimental procedure be applied with any real cogency to any hypothesis about him. He cannot satisfy the requirements to rank as an empirically detectable object.

What are these requirements in detail? On what conditions can an object, itself unobservable, become known to us by inference from what we observe? Three conditions seem necessary and sufficient:

(1) The object inferred must be of a clearly defined character, not just a something in general. If we do not know *what* we are inferring, our knowledge is not advanced at all.

(2) The inference must rest upon definite evidence, not upon some impression about things in general. We must be able to say what precisely we offer as our evidence for it. This evidence must consist in observations which can be intelligibly and unambiguously

described and inferences which can be intelligibly and unambiguously set out for all interested persons. It must be possible to repeat the observations at will, or if not, then to make others which tend to confirm them.

(3) Our inference must be the only reasonable explanation of the facts, or at least the most reasonable explanation that we can conceive.

What are the facts of experience from which the existence of God is with some seeming plausibility inferred? An intelligent being, such as God is supposed to be, is most readily traced by his actions. Such an inference is often made in historical studies and in detective work. One finds among one's data a set of facts which seems to invite interpretation in terms of an agent previously unknown to us. In the case of God the evidence lies overwhelmingly in the seeming traces of purpose in nature, most strikingly in the long record of the evolution of life and mind. To this may be added the record of progress in intellectual and moral achievement which stands out from the pages of history. Given that nature on the purely physical level seems so lifeless and mindless, it is argued that the steady growth of life and mind within such a universe is evidence for an intelligent purposive agency which is not that of nature, but capable of projecting its purposes upon nature and working them out there. Into this overall picture can be inserted from each person's experience particular events which have a providential look, whether in the life of an individual or of a larger group such as a nation.[1]

For a God-belief founded on arguments such as these, it is sometimes claimed that an experimental verification is possible. From one's conception of God one deduces certain directives for conduct and lives one's life according to these directives. In course of time one finds one's ideas of God and man becoming clearer, and one sees more and more of the signs of God's guiding action in events as one becomes better able to detect them. If a community lives its life according to the directives, it will find its community life strengthened and purified. The individual will find, if he is of the

---

[1] I do not add to the list occurrences of the kind called miraculous (in the strict sense of the word), although there are people who believe that such occurrences take place. In the thought-atmosphere of today such stories are evidential only to those who already believe in God, and not by any means to all even of them. They are therefore no part of that common experience of mankind, upon which a theism that is to be an empirical discipline must rest.

responsive kind, that he enters into a kind of intimacy or fellowship with God and, by reflex from this, with others around him.

In passing it may be said that this kind of claim is more easily made for a particular religion than for a bare generalised theism. The particular religion will have a fuller conception of God, a detailed set of directives ready made, a way of moral and spiritual discipline and a traditional account of the kind of experiences which are to be expected as one follows it; in a word, something more specific to do and something more specific to verify. There will also be the community's experience to draw upon; for all religious communities keep up the memory of the experiences of their members, and an adherent is often prepared to take on trust, until it verifies itself in his own life, the experience of those who have gone further along the road before him. An unattached theist is unlikely to enter so intimately into any of these bodies of recorded experience.

Nevertheless the attempt to build theism as a body of empirical knowledge on foundations like these cannot succeed.

(1) God cannot be precisely and unambiguously defined, nor can his relation to the empirical world, either in terms of possible observations or in terms of a theoretical system capable of precise correlation with observables. The indefiniteness of much which we say about him will become a major issue for us later on. For the moment let us recognise it and pass on.

(2) The claim to verify predictions experimentally can only be made plausible by using the word 'experiment' in a very loose sense. Nothing like what science means by experimentation is possible in this field. We cannot define precisely the terms of a hypothesis, or deduce with rigour and precision the consequences flowing from it. We cannot mount an experiment under controlled conditions, or carry out a planned run of experiments to test a theory in depth. There is no precise reporting of results. Moreover, a proper scientific experiment should take a limited time to carry out, and then the result is known; but the evidence to which the theist appeals is the experience of a life-time, and that goes on indefinitely and cannot be fully known or assessed until life is over. While it is always possible to say that one will know the result in the next life, that seems rather late, and the outlook for the enquirer in this life is bleak.

(3) It being thus impossible to perform determinate experiments to settle determinate points, an empirically grounded theism can be no more in the end than a general impression derived from a more or

less detailed survey of common experience. And here two further difficulties have to be faced. First, the facts for which a theist interpretation is offered will always be found to be capable of at least one non-theist interpretation. Second, there is a huge mass of counter-evidence: dysteleology, wrong turns in animal evolution and in human history, particular events in which a kind of anti-providence, a kind of mischief-making force seems to be at work, death and suffering, ill will among human beings, the gross disparity between moral merit and good fortune or happiness. In face of all this, the theist has two recourses, neither of which is free from difficulties of its own.

(a) He may counterbalance the sufferings and the moral and spiritual evil by saying that all will be redressed in a future life; but such a contention is verifiable only in that life, and such post-mortem verification is not acceptable by ordinary empiricist standards.

(b) He may qualify the meaning of what he says. For example, he usually claims that God is good in himself and good to men; but there are numerous instances of what to an unenlightened eye appear to be his cruelty and his injustice. The theist replies that God gives us what is really good for us, not what we like or wish, and that it is our sense of values which needs to be corrected. But this can only mean in the end that the meaning of 'good' is stretched to cover anything that God may do; and then the theist's statement that God is good becomes true by definition but completely uninformative. I do not overlook the sincerity and intense devotion of some who have taken this line, accepting whatever comes and calling it good just because it is what comes; indeed, I am sure it has much to tell us about what lies at the heart of religion; but it is not a strong contribution to the building up of a reasoned case for theism.

Theological assertions, then, by empiricist standards, cannot be known to be true. They are speculations which may perhaps have some value as imaginative fiction, but they have no cognitive value at all.

THE QUESTION OF MEANINGFULNESS

What I have said so far in this chapter could have been said by anyone in the empiricist tradition at any time in the last century or two; but in the last forty years a new note has entered into the discussion. Because theological assertions are not empirically verifiable, they have been declared to be meaningless. This contention was given wide currency among English-language readers by A. J. Ayer in his book *Language, Truth and Logic* (1936), and the debate which it set going has never completely died down. Ayer's book was not directed only against theology, but against ethical and metaphysical discourse as well, convicting all these of meaninglessness and calling for radical changes in the practice of philosophy. The theological aspect of Ayer's challenge was reinforced in 1950 by A. G. N. Flew in a paper on 'Theology and Falsification', which led to an interesting discussion among philosophers and theologians. Ayer and Flew present the same challenge, though in slightly different ways. Both give prominence to the issue of the verifiability or falsifiability, i.e. the experimental testability, of theological utterances. Both maintain that because theological utterances are not definite enough to satisfy the proper empirical tests, they cannot be said to have any cognitive meaning, whatever value they may have as expressions of feelings and aspirations.

The use of the word 'meaningless' by Ayer and others gave offence to many, who did not mind being told that what they said was untrue, but resented being told that they were only making meaningless noises. It sounded like deliberate rudeness, and we need not deny that it was meant to be provocative. But in fact the word is capable of an interpretation which need not ruffle anyone's feelings, and yet embodies an intellectual challenge of which notice must be taken.

Ayer presents his contention as a consequence of the verifiability principle, which (as he interprets it) means that no utterance purporting to be a statement of fact can be meaningful unless it is possible to point to some fact of experience which, if it occurred, would serve to establish the truth of the statement as probable. It is not necessary, for a statement to be meaningful, that we should be actually in possession of the evidence which verifies it; but it is necessary that we should know what facts of experience would verify the statement, if we were to observe them. If it is not possible to specify what experimental evidence would constitute a verification of the statement, we do not know what it means, and in fact it means nothing.

The verifiability principle comes originally from the logical positivist school, of which a great deal was heard in this country in the years between 1930 and 1950. In the heyday of that school the principle was much discussed and often formulated and refor-mulated. No formulation of it found general acceptance, and it is not a standard slogan of present-day empiricism; but it stands for something, and we must see what that something is.

Logical positivism arose at a time of radical change in the physical sciences. Entities such as absolute space and time, absolute motion and velocity, and the luminiferous ether, which had been essential components of the theoretical system of physics, were being abolished because they were undetectable by any experiment that could be devised. Physics is an empirical science, and cannot recognise the existence of things for which there is no empirical evidence. It is not necessary, for a thing to be acceptable in physical theory, that that thing should itself be observable; but there must be some observable fact, some experimentally obtainable result, which is consistent with the thing's being a reality and would be different if the thing were not a reality. Any alleged entity which does not authenticate itself in this way, any alleged entity whose existence cannot be checked by observation and experiment, is to be regarded as physically meaningless. Ether and absolute space and the rest were found to be physically meaningless; they were rejected and the science was reconstructed without them.

There was also a tendency among the philosophers to get rid of purely theoretical, unobservable entities, even where the working scientist was satisfied, on the evidence, to incorporate them in his theory. Everything was to be redefined in terms of what is actually observed, and so a really radical empiricism was to be achieved.

Logical positivism interpreted natural science in this way and took it, so interpreted, as the model of what knowledge should be. The common-sense thinking of the ordinary man was a primitive, methodologically unselfconscious form of science. The underlying principles of both were the same, and no intellectual exercise which did not conform to these principles could be recognised as leading to knowledge. Other functions it might have, as an expression of feelings and attitudes, as command or precept or exhortation, and these might be important and valuable functions in their own way, but whatever value they had it was not knowledge-value. This was expressed by saying that utterances of that kind were meaningless, by which was meant scientifically meaningless; no other kind of meaning really interested the logical positivists. Of course, in the ordinary use of language, expressions of feeling, commands, exhortations and the like are not called meaningless; for they can be understood, interpreted, discussed. But they are not part of reality-thinking, they make no contribution to our knowledge of what exists, a scientist can make no use of them in his work. They are scientifically meaningless, and that is the point. Logical positivism was an attempt to state a fundamental rule for scientific thinking while also declaring it to be a rule for all possible reality-thinking.

The verifiability principle is capable of a stricter and a looser interpretation. According to the stricter interpretation, no statement is meaningful unless its content is a description of observables, or can be reduced to a set of statements which are descriptions of observables. It is verified by our actually observing the observables to which it directly or indirectly refers. That is how it came to be accepted doctrine that 'the meaning of a proposition is the means of its verification'; the facts of experience which are what the proposition asserts are the facts by observing which we verify the proposition, and if we wish to know what the proposition means or asserts, it is enough to know how to verify it.

The verifiability principle, thus interpreted, rules out standard theism. The standard account of 'God' cannot be reduced to a set of directions bidding us make certain observations. It has indeed been suggested that 'God exists' might be reducible to 'people sometimes have experiences which they call encounters with God'. But it is generally recognised that theism means more than this; it means that the experiences in question really are encounters with a God who really is there to be encountered. Besides, theism says much more about God than that we have experiences in which we say we encounter him. It really cannot be reconciled with the verifiability principle in its strict form.

But neither can the common use of language. To people who are not tied to a philosophical school, it seems obvious that the meaning of a proposition is not to be identified with the means of its verification, and furthermore that it is possible to verify a proposition (not decisively, but well enough to be going on with) without actually observing that to which the proposition refers. All that is necessary is to be able to observe facts of experience which are to be expected if the proposition is true and not if it is false. If any form of the verifiability principle is to be accepted, therefore, it must be the looser form: no statement is meaningful unless there is something in experience which will be different according as the statement is true or false, something which counts as evidence in support of the statement and invests it with a degree of probability.

Ayer accepted and used the principle in this its looser form, and claimed in so doing to be no mere follower of a recent fashion, but to be in line with the centuries-old English tradition of empiricism. And he set out, as Hume had done in his time, to show that the serious acceptance of empiricism means a revolution in philosophy. For there still survives in some places the ancient metaphysical tradition, which holds that discoveries can be made about the real nature of things by methods which are not those of empirical science; it also holds that value-judgments are in some sense discoveries of reality. Philosophers should realise that these traditional views and the methods and procedures associated with them must be cast aside. Little will then remain of what used to be called 'philosophy' except logic and an empiricist theory of knowledge.

What applies to metaphysics applies also to theology. Statements about 'God' are not expressible in terms which science can use, or verifiable by what science can recognise as being evidence. For God is no component of that world of sensible objects, parts of which are constantly under our observation; nor can the contention that he exists and operates in certain ways be stated as an intelligible scientific hypothesis. In sum, it is the empiricist critique of theism as we stated it before, only with the added feature that the rejected doctrine is declared to be not merely unproven, not merely false, but meaningless.

Theism had its defenders, of course. Some of them, thinking not only of Ayer but of all that lies behind him, attacked the verifiability principle, which in its stricter interpretation it was not difficult to do. But it was, and is, less easy to evade what lay behind the principle, viz. the vast difference in character between theological thinking and empirical scientific thinking, with the implications of that for the status and significance of theology.

Some, again, attacked the use of the word 'meaningless'. It was easy to point out that there are other kinds of meaningfulness besides scientific meaningfulness. Value-judgments, exhortations, commands, promises and the like all have their own kinds of meaning. We know how to react to them, and what reactions to expect from other people when we ourselves give utterance in these forms. But that does not rid us of the peculiar problem about theological statements, which is that they are intended as a kind of statements of fact, as an account of existing realities. They cannot be fobbed off with the concession of those other kinds of meaning; they claim cognitive meaning, and how can they have it?

We are experiencing a revolution today not only in philosophy, but in our whole culture. We tend more and more to regard science as the paradigm of what knowledge really means, and it becomes harder and harder to give the name of knowledge to metaphysical or theological assertions, even though we may be committed to making these assertions and convinced that they are in some way right and proper assertions to make. Thinking this, we still wonder what we are really doing when we make them. What is the force of the assertorial form in which we cast our theological utterances, and what is our justification for using what sounds so like the language of factual knowledge when that is not what we have? Can there be some kind of reality-thinking which is distinct from the investigation of existing fact? What could be meant by 'reality' or 'truth' in such a connection?

One thing at any rate we must recognise: that God-belief has two features which an empiricist account of it cannot explain. (a) God is thought of not merely as a great and benevolent power, but as the Absolute, as Being itself, incommensurable with any of the finite beings which owe their existence to him. This may not be obvious if we treat God merely as an object of speculation, but it is obvious as soon as we see 'God' in the proper religious context. For it is this absoluteness and incommensurability in him which evoke the characteristic response of worship. (b) Belief in God is not held as a hypothesis, subject to constant re-checking and exposed to the ultimate possibility of falsification. It is held as an unquestionable certitude. I do not of course mean that no God-believer can ever change his mind and cease to believe, but that the 'feel' of the belief, while it is held, is different from that of any scientific theory. It is the prior presence of this conviction which gives persuasiveness to the empirical evidences, so weak and dubious in themselves.

Empirical arguments will never yield this. What can, if not metaphysical theology? What that is, and how it works, we shall see later on; and then it in turn will reveal its inherent weakness. Meanwhile the insistent probing from the empiricist side has yet more to reveal to us, and that shall be the subject of another chapter.

3 The Elusiveness of Theological Statements

The discussion arising from Flew's paper of 1950 raises the issue of the 'meaningfulness' of theological utterances in a sense nearer to the ordinary use of the word. He complains that we can never know definitely what theists mean by what they say, because when faced with awkward arguments or facts of experience (such as the fact of evil in the world, which seems to cast doubt on the alleged goodness of God) they alter the meanings of their words, and you can never pin them down. They say that God is good, just, loving; and the course of events in the world contains much which, to an outsider, seems incompatible with this assertion. But the theists are strangely unmoved by what, to the non-theist, seems so clear a case. They say that God's conduct is not to be judged by the same standards which we apply to one another, and they insist that he is behaving justly and lovingly even where it seems clear that he is doing nothing of the kind. Nothing seems to count, in their eyes, as a refutation of their claims about him. And Flew argues that an assertion of God's goodness which is elastic enough to cover what we actually find him doing is too elastic to mean anything at all. He challenges the theists to say what they would accept as a refutation of their assertions; for we cannot know what these mean until we know at least what would be incompatible with them. Theists, in a word, are invited to show that their assertions do mean something by showing how they could be falsified.

Flew is here using the up-do-date falsifiability ploy to make a point which in itself is not novel. It is the age-old problem of evil, which is endemic in all theist systems. God is to be conceived as the sole ultimate source and ground of all that is and happens in the world; he is also to be conceived as absolutely wise and absolutely good. In his world, then, how is evil even possible? And granting it to be possible, how can he allow it to become actual? Conversely, since evil is undeniably actual, in what conceivable sense can God be said to be good?

24

THE PROBLEM OF EVIL AND THE 'GOODNESS' OF GOD

The standard doctrine is that God is altogether good, which means both good in himself, possessing in his own being unlimited and unqualified joy, and good in relation to us, that is to say, just, loving and kind. How then are we to account for the vast amount of unmerited suffering in the world arising from natural causes, i.e. causes which are built into the structure of the universe? And how account for the enormity of evil will in man, and the endless suffering and injustice which arises from it? Is God under a constraint, unwilling to allow evil but unable to prevent it? But he is the sole source of all that is and happens; what could constrain him? Is he lacking in wisdom, unable for that reason to contrive the kind of world he would wish? But how can the All-Designer fail to understand his own work? If he is the source and origin of all being, how can he give existence to anything which he does not thoroughly understand? But if he is not lacking in power or in wisdom, what becomes of his goodness?

Among Christians it is considered wrong to say that God is the author of evil; and conventional Christian teaching tries to rid him of the responsibility at any rate for moral evil and its consequences by saying that he has endowed his intelligent creatures with free will. This, it is said, entails for them the capacity to sin, and it also entails that the responsibility for their sin is not God's but theirs. This however will not do; for God in creating the world acted under no constraint and under no misapprehension. He knew it was a world in which these things could and would happen, and he could have prevented them from happening simply by not creating it. And if he could have prevented it and did not, how can he not have a certain moral responsibility for it? And then too there is all the suffering which does not arise from man's sin, but seems to result directly from the structure of the universe. Whose is the responsibility for that? In short, the free-will ploy does not do what it was brought in to do. The Jewish, Christian and Muslim scriptures all have the insight and the courage to declare that God is indeed the sole Creator of all that is and happens, be it good or evil.

There is one sense, nevertheless, in which theism must say that evil is not God's work, namely that it is not, like other created things, a true and faithful, though finite, reflection of his nature. It is more like his opposite, in so far as an opposite to God can exist at all; and in giving it existence God is calling into existence the negation of himself. Not for its own sake, we may suppose, but for the sake of the dramatic struggle in which he means to engage with it; and we cannot expect to understand it except by seeing it in that context, as part of a design in which its malice is somehow finally cancelled and the opposition overcome. But in our experience in this life we do not detect such a design. At best we may think we catch a glimpse of it in favoured moments; and even this we can only do in the light of some particular religious and theological tradition. Natural theology cannot give this flash of insight.

Yet it can lay down two lines which thought can follow in the search for it.

The first is to call in another world, another life, to redress the balance of the present one. This can be a satisfactory answer on certain conditions: the present innocent sufferer, on reaching the future life and looking back upon his experiences here in the fresh light which he will then have, must be prepared himself to acknowledge the goodness of the whole sequence, seen as a whole. If that condition is not satisfied, there is no genuine compensation for what he now suffers, but only a putting to sleep of the memory of injustice. But to one outside the faith, of course, this enormous draft upon a postulated future is likely to be beyond all credibility.

That line of thought preserves the possibility of understanding God to be just and loving in something like the accepted use of these words, but at the cost of a hypothesis which no one can verify or falsify in this life. The second line of thought is more radical. It challenges our standards of judgment and says that it is our own values and our own selves that need revision. In itself this is nothing strange. We know how in ordinary life our value-judgments do change with growing experience. As we learn more about the facts of life, and our attitudes change with increasing maturity, so we change our conception of what is important, what is worth while, even of what is just. These changes are an inescapable part of growing older, but the form they take is affected by what we really care about; and if what we really care about is God and a certain kind of relationship with God, that will affect the way in which we mature. A time may come when we are glad to surrender ourselves to him to do as he will with us, when events are the medium of a kind of communication, even of a kind of love-play between him and us, and no thought of rights or claims or justice or the like can any longer arise. Even suffering becomes acceptable just because it comes from him, without our wishing to see the further perspective of his design. If the rough treatment to which he subjects us brings us to the point of seeing our own insignificance, and forgetting ourselves in total oblation to him, it is thereby fully justified.[1]

There is here still a formal likeness to the ordinary understanding of God's goodness. There is a concept of what is good, viz. God in himself and the maintenance on our part of a certain relationship with him. To say that God is good to us, on this view, really means that God makes it possible for us to reach and maintain this relationship. It is only that there has been a shift in what we most care about, and therefore in what we think to be good.

Perhaps these two lines of thought are necessary to one another, so that only a combination of the two will give us a plausible solution to our problem. For (a) the second line of thought is well enough for the devotee who understands it and finds satisfaction in embracing it. But in this life he is in a minority, and on a broad view this solution will not work unless everyone who suffers in this life is ultimately brought to see it; which must necessarily happen in another life, since it evidently does not happen here. Thus the postulate of an after-life is unavoidable. And on the other hand (b) our first line of thought required that all sufferers should, here or hereafter, come to a point where they could frankly acknowledge the goodness of God's dealings with them, sufferings and all; and if we ask from what point of view they could conceivably come to think this, our second line of thought offers the only plausible answer.

The second line of thought is characteristic of those who go more deeply into the secret places of their religion than do most. To them its truth and finality seem evident. But if this is indeed the meaning of 'God is good', it is bound to be puzzling as well as unconvincing to all who have not arrived at a certain degree of experience in the Godward life. That does not mean that it cannot be a correct interpretation, but, if it is so, it carries the consequence that the goodness of God is an esoteric doctrine, at home within a worshipping community, but liable to be misunderstood in the

[1] Cf. Ramon Lull, *The Book of the Lover and the Beloved*, 7: The Beloved asked the Lover, 'Hast thou remembrance of anything with which I have rewarded thee, that thou wouldst love me thus?' 'Yea,' replied the Lover, 'for I distinguish not between the trials that thou sendest me and the joys.' 8: 'Say, O Lover,' asked the Beloved, 'if I double thy trials, wilt thou still be patient?' 'Yea,' answered the Lover, 'so that thou double also my love.'

world at large. If that is the case, it is at any rate some gain to have got it established.

But not all members of the worshipping community itself would show a firm grasp of all this. For, after all, these are things to which we have to grow up, and the worshipping community at any given time will contain many members who are not fully mature. Two points may be made in this connection. (a) Understanding can sometimes come in advance of maturity. It is possible to have an intellectual insight into certain things at a quite early stage of development, long years before this insight becomes woven into the substance of one's thought and life. On the other hand (b) the believer's growth in understanding does not necessarily mean that he becomes a philosopher or an analytical theologian. Much may go on in the unconscious, leading to intuitive realisations, and finding expression very likely in imagery rather than in clear-out statements. Some such process may be taken to be going on in the minds of many who are serious believers in God, without being analytical thinkers.

PECULIARITIES OF RELIGIOUS UTTERANCE

The difficulty of pinning down the meaning of statements about God has been known to theists for hundreds and even thousands of years, and their attempts to deal with it are incorporated in the theological tradition. It involves more problems and more kinds of problems than Flew mentions, though his is one of the most obtrusive and one of the most troublesome to deal with.

Flew's problem is that of a statement, 'God is good', which has at first sight an easily intelligible meaning, but which in its obvious sense comes into conflict with facts of experience. It therefore has to be interpreted, and there lies the difficulty. But sometimes difficulty arises from assertions which cannot be true of God if he is what he is defined to be – as when spatial location is ascribed to him, or he is treated as subject to change, or as having passions which even in a human being would be considered unworthy. And behind all this there is the characteristic indirectness of religious expression, where so often we convey one thing by saying another.

Religion has a peculiar style of speech and self-expression. Many of its best-known and most characteristic verbal utterances are couched in a figurative style, indirect and allusive. Simile is frequent, metaphor much more frequent, and in some religious writings extensive use is made of parable and of allegory. When we try to analyse and get behind the metaphors, very often what we arrive at is itself again metaphorical. Like poetic expression, religious discourse can sometimes be several layers deep in figurativeness.

This peculiarity of religious expression has perhaps something to do with the way in which religious truth, or what is believed to be such, is apprehended. It comes more usually as an intuitive realisation than as a reasoned conclusion, and it is natural that the expression of an intuitive insight should be imaginative in form. The religious mind can analyse in its own way when it wishes to do so, in meditation, in preparing a sermon, in writing theology; but its primary mode of utterence is not analytical. Add to this that the matters of which religion speaks are linked with the most deep-rooted hopes and fears of the human soul, such as find expression in a different way through poetry and the other arts. We can thus understand why so much primary religious expression takes the form of singing and dancing and ritual performances, of image-making and temple-building, of hymns and religious poetry. There is hardly a religious system in the world in which activities like these do not play an important part. Even where a movement arises in criticism of and rebellion against these things, where the images are swept away and the ceremonies cut down to their bare minimum in the interests of a 'spiritual' approach to God, the movement finds its own forms of expression, and they are in a similar mode. The Protestants who abolished images and wall-paintings from their churches poured themselves out in psalmody and hymnody and religious music. The Quaker silence has itself something of a ritual quality, and the Quaker way of life in its heyday was stylised in such matters as speech and dress.

But that is not all. The peculiar form of religious expression has also something to do with the nature of what is expressed. Religion deals with things to which human thought and speech are not well geared. It takes man in his most mysterious aspect, in the depths of his spiritual life and in his relations with 'God', and pursues him beyond death into a supposed new mode of existence which is beyond the range of empirical study. It speaks of God himself, who is not merely inaccessible to observation and experiment, but in his nature radically different from everything of which we have experience. Yet we have no terms in which to speak of God except such as we have forged for use in speaking of empirical objects. We have to do the best we can with these terms; and though we know they are always inadequate, sometimes far-fetched and sometimes misleading, we have no way of correcting a faulty expression except by setting beside it another expression which will itself be faulty. It is not surprising if our efforts to work in such a medium result in indirection, complexity and paradox.

PROBLEMS OF INTERPRETATION

Problems arise only where there is doubt as to the meaning of what is said. Often there is no doubt. Some theological statements are so obviously figurative that no one in his senses could think otherwise, and at the same time so clear that no one can doubt what they mean. When God is said to be a sun and shield, a rock or a fortress, the point of the comparison is clear and no more need be said.

It is more complex when Christ is called the Lamb. That needs some background knowledge about early customs and theological ideas. On seeking this knowledge we find that more than one religious rite involving the slaughter of lambs has contributed to the meaning, and more than one aspect of the religious significance of such rites. The character of the lamb itself, as an animal possessing certain qualities, also counts for something. The image is like a material which displays different colours when held up in different ways to the light; and it is not likely that anyone using the image on a particular occasion consciously intends all its possible shades of meaning. And when all that has been sorted out, and we know to what kind of lamb in what kind of context Christ is being likened, we have still to ask what this multivalent comparison is meant to tell us about him, since he is not literally a lamb and was not slaughtered as part of a religious rite.

It is much the same when we are dealing with a parable, i.e. a story of an action, usually performed by a human agent, which is supposed to tell us by analogy something about God. Here again we may find ourselves with a problem on two levels. First of all there is the story which constitutes the parable: a father welcomes home his estranged but repentant son and rebukes his churlish brother; a feudal lord cancels a great debt, but revokes the cancellation and proceeds against the debtor with the utmost rigour when it appears that he will not do anything to relieve his own debtors; and so on. It is clear God is not really a householder who has two sons, or a lord who has judicial power over his debtors. What is attributed to God is the action, or something in the action, performed by these characters. But then we may find ourselves wondering what can be meant by ascribing such an action to God. Christianity has a lot to say about judgment, condemnation and forgiveness as actions performed by God; but what actually is it for God to judge a man, or to condemn, or to forgive? We who inherit the Christian tradition talk of these things as if their meaning were clear; but is it? Suppose, for example, we are asked what is the relation between God's judgment on a man and the man's own judgment upon himself, or how God's judgment is declared (in this life at least) otherwise than through the man's own critical self-consciousness. And suppose it is suggested that the drama of guilt, conviction, forgiveness and reconciliation, which plays so central a part in Christian teaching, is nothing other than the story of the dissolution of an over-rigorous super-ego and the establishment of a balance whereby the soul can come to terms with itself as it is. If there is truth in these suggestions, what is left in the judgment and forgiveness doctrines that can be attributed to God? Or, if the Christian teaching on this subject does not mean what is here suggested, what does it mean?

Some God-statements cannot be seen by simple inspection to be figurative, but are in conflict with other theological propositions which have to be given precedence. Such are the numerous anthropomorphisms with which religious language is shot through, and the expressions which use spatio-temporal terms for things which in deep doctrine are not spatio-temporal.

Thus God is supposed to have a dwelling-place, which is called heaven and is conventionally 'above' the dwelling-places of man. Spatially this is nonsense; there is no locality which can be so described. Theologically too it is nonsense, for God is not subject to spatial location at all. The inner meaning of this language and the reason for its persistence can only be seen by one who understands the ontological dimension in which the great scale of being is constructed. One who has been inoculated against this understanding (an operation nowadays often successfully performed) will be helpless here.

Space and time are both involved in the Christian myth of the Incarnation. Christ, who existed beforehand in heaven in enjoyment of the glories of deity, divested himself of his glory, came down from heaven to earth and became man, and afterwards ascended from earth to heaven, where he now is and will always be. This is dramatically a good story, but theologically it is impossible. For who or what came from heaven to earth? Not the human nature of Christ, for that never existed until it was created in the womb of Mary. Not his divine nature, for that did not leave heaven or lay aside its deity; the whole point of the story is that he who walked the earth, being truly and entirely man, was at the same time truly and entirely God. Nor can even the divine nature of Christ strictly be said to have existed before the Incarnation, except from a purely human-historical point of view, since it is not subject to time. So the whole thrilling story dissolves (under the acids of Christian theology itself, be it noted) into – what? What do those who assert it really mean? What is a valid analysis of their myth? As to the Ascension with which the story closes, it is enough to say that is shares in all the difficulties which are inherent in the idea of heaven as a place to which people can go and where they can live.

GOD'S MORAL CHARACTER AGAIN

What most of all concerns us, and weighs upon the minds of multitudes who are not philosophers or theologians, is the question of the moral character which religious teaching in general ascribes to God.

He is credited with passions about whose worthiness we have doubts even when they occur in men. For example, he is jealous, exclusively self-assertive, avid of praise and unconditional devotion. In man that is certainly wrong. It could be argued that it is not wrong in God because he is not, like a man, one among many who are all his peers, but unique and incomparable; it could also be argued that it is good for us to know this, and therefore it is good that God should keep reminding us of it. It is fair to say that the more reflective of our religious guides do sometimes try to explain things in this way.

Or again, God is prone to anger. He is angry when human beings do what does not meet with his approval, and his anger leads to punitive action and in extreme cases to final damnation. In Christianity he is said to have made complex arrangements in order to enable himself to pardon offenders without relaxing his inflexible standards; but the many rival versions of the Christian 'plan of salvation' include at least some to which objection can be taken on moral grounds. Here again we must in fairness acknowledge that anger is not necessarily an unworthy state of mind. There are times when one does well to be angry. There is a truly disinterested anger which one can feel towards someone who obstinately refuses to do what is best for himself – which e.g. a nurse or a doctor may feel towards an intractable patient. And if, as the theologians would agree, to do as God bids us is in fact the true and only way to secure our own ultimate welfare, and that is part of his motive in bidding us do it, then God may well be thought to be angry in that disinterested way when we refuse to follow his directions. In that case his anger would be merely an expression of his goodness. One wishes that this were explicitly and unmistakably said, and that religious teaching and literature contained fewer apparent echoes of a primitive and barbarous super-ego. Is it perhaps because the religious community does not know its own meaning, but goes on compulsively repeating its ambiguous formulae while leaving everyone to interpret them according to his own wisdom or folly?

These are moral considerations and moral interpretation; but metaphysical points also arise. What are we to suppose is meant by ascribing passions to God, quite apart from the moral quality of the passions? For a passion is a passivity, a response triggered off by a cause acting upon the subject who feels the passion. But God has no experiences of that kind. Nor for that matter can he be credited with a sense of justice at all like ours, which is to us an ideal and a law to which we feel ourselves subject. At the end of the day there seems to be small profit in trying to describe experiences of a sort which could plausibly be ascribed to God. Better to recognise outright that we are in no position to write a theopsychology, or analyse God's inner life, or try to imagine what kind of experience could, in God's life, occupy a place analogous to that held by e.g. anger or love or pity in ours. It is wiser, because more circumspect, to say that when we speak of God's anger or love or pity we mean some of his actions, which are analogous in certain definite ways to acts performed by the angry or loving or compassionate man.

This behaviourist interpretation of statements ascribing experiences and personal qualities to God is the only one which is definite enough to be seriously discussed. It is the one in terms of which Flew shapes his challenge in the matter of the goodness of God; it is for good conduct on God's part that he looks, and looks in vain. And yet this is not the whole of what standard theism means. Standard theism certainly means that behind God's actions as seen in the world of our experience there is God's own inherent life, which is an experience of unqualified joy and splendour – 'glory' in religious language. The difficulties which we meet in trying to conceive it will concern us again in Chapter 7.

INDEFINABILITY AND FLEXIBILITY

The problem of the interpretation of theological statements has evidently many aspects, most of which arise from the fact that there is no vocabulary of terms with definite meanings for use in application to 'God'. All that we say is figurative, analogical, symbolic, and the interpretation of the symbols can never be fixed. But there is advantage in this very fact of symbolic language – the advantage of flexibility. For the same symbol can have more than one significant aspect; and it can be significant on more than one level, intellectual or emotional, so that it can appeal to a variety of people and have something to say to all of them. One can analyse the meaning of a symbolic action or of a figurative utterance, one can find in it several strands of meaning and still be left feeling that there is more to be said. The images are charged with a wealth of meaning which perhaps was never all together in the conscious mind of any one person.

Of course there are difficulties too. Some people are less at home with figurative expression than others, and what inspires one may leave another puzzled and suspicious. The same symbol may strike different people with very different emotional force. Images may lose something of their power if they are carried over into a culture which does not know the objects from which they are drawn, or which knows them with different associations. And most images contain some element of inherent ambiguity, whence arise misunderstandings that may harden into heresies and schisms. Thus it has long been debatable among Christians how literally certain words and images in their conventional story are to be taken – e.g. words and images relating to the Ascension of Christ, to the presence of Christ in the Eucharist, or to the doctrine of his atoning death.

And yet this kind of difficulty may well seem greater to the outsider than to one who is at home in the particular religion concerned. Where a tradition of this kind of language has gone on for a few centuries, with the principal images and symbols continually repeated, reflected upon, compared and combined, there comes into existence a network of associations and cross-references which only those who are at home in the tradition can fully trace. None of the images can be safely interpreted in isolation. Each is an analogy, and all analogies are imperfect. One is always in danger of misinterpreting an analogy by taking as part of its meaning one of those aspects which one is meant to discount. The method commonly used to forestall this kind of mistake is to play off image against image, so that what is false in one image is contradicted by another, while they reinforce and support one another in those points which are to be taken as valid. Thus it is only by taking all of them together that their true interpretation can be safeguarded. It is not one or two privileged images, but all of them taken together in their coherence, that express the mind of the religion to which they belong.

There is here a fascinating field of study. Religious language has many features in common with the language of poetry; the same prevalence of metaphor, analogy and other forms of indirect expression, the same depth of symbolic meaning attaching to the images used, the same emotional power, the same capacity to be meaningful on several different levels at once. But religious utterances are supposed to be about objective realities in a sense in which poetic utterances are not, and are further supposed to be reducible within a consistent body of theological principles. Here is a border-line field of study between aesthetics and philosophy of religion. But we must resist the temptation to go further into it. We are concerned with it only in relation to our proper theme: the varying usages of the term 'God'.

This figurative character of religious expression, this ambiguity, this power of holding many meanings in one symbol, is a great help in the process by which the mind of the believer slowly grows towards a mature understanding of his belief. It allows different views to coexist; the same symbol can be taken in a crude and primitive sense, but also in a reflective and refined sense, at one and the same time in the same religious community, and at different times in the history of the same mind. Changes of emphasis and of interpretation can thus come about unfelt and unnoticed in the course of a healthy growth. Two consequences follow, however, which are of interest to the philosophical observer. (a) There is no one interpretation of theological expressions which is *the* meaning of them. For each expression there is a sliding scale of possible meanings. They are not to be approached like philosophical or scientific statements, but studied in a more flexible and imaginative way. (b) The more sophisticated an interpretation is, the less likely it is to suggest itself, or even to be intelligible, except to initiates or to those who have put in an amount of study which gives them a quasi-initiation.

4 Standard and Non-standard Usages of 'God'

Theology is clearly not knowledge as that word is used in modern logic. It is not knowledge as knowledge is exemplified in empirical science. So obviously is this the case, that one is led to ask why anyone should spend time and effort on theology. It presents itself on a first view as a set of assertions about real existence; but on inspection we find it impossible to understand what it asserts or to discover what right it has to assert it. Why is it still kept alive?

Not out of a purely theoretical interest. As a purely theoretical enquiry, theology is a non-starter. Nor is there any doubt what gives it its continuing life. It is the religious interest. If we are to press on further with the analysis of 'God', we shall find that religion insists on being part of the theme.

Yet not every form or aspect of religion; only those forms and aspects of religion which centre upon 'God', and these are not the whole. There are in fact uses of the word 'God' which are not religious, and there are forms of religion which do not centre upon 'God'. These are not what may be called the standard uses of 'God' or the standard forms of religion, but they have their importance, and merit our attention for a while before we set them aside and move into the heart of the matter.

NON-RELIGIOUS USAGES OF 'GOD'

It is an old and well-established custom in certain contexts to use God-language while not intending to assert the existence of any divine being distinct from nature and the processes of nature. In our own society anyone can see that the personalist language in which we speak of God is often used in a very attenuated sense. It is never used meaninglessly, except in profane swearing. But often when 'God' is spoken of, what is meant seems to be merely those things in

nature or in the course of history which are beyond our control and
perhaps our understanding, but which determine our destinies for
good or ill. We are helpless in face of them, we are reduced to
tremulous hope or silent acceptance, and these are attitudes which
partly resemble those of the believer in face of the acts of his God. So
we may use God's name in speaking of such things, without at all
wishing to be understood as affirming any theological propositions.
Statements about God can be a literary form in which to express
views on the nature of the universe and of man, on history and
human fortune, on moral and other values. Participation in public
acts of worship can be a conventional (but not therefore meaningless) way of declaring our recognition of the importance of these
things, a way of proclaiming that man is not exempt from the laws of
the universe, or free to act as he chooses without having to abide the
consequences. Such a usage has been tacitly recognised and widely
practised in ancient as well as in modern times.

A legal document speaks of certain accidents as 'acts of God'. It
would be naïve to suppose that anyone is committed thereby to a
theological interpretation of what has happened. All that is meant is
that no human agent can be held responsible for it.

A philosopher, a self-proclaimed materialist, criticises the speculative metaphysicians who think they have got the secret of all
reality in some system of ideas of their own devising. Borrowing
language from Spinoza, he says to them, 'I do not believe you, God
is great'. He means, of course, that the variety of manifestations of
being of which the universe is capable is beyond any human
formula, and that this fact demands a certain respect, a certain
modesty and self-restraint, on the part of the metaphysician. He
even rejoices in this escape from finite human fancies into the
infinity of real being.

A poet, watching the public rejoicings on the occasion of a royal
Jubilee, and reflecting on the oft-repeated words 'God save the
Queen', addresses the people:

> Get you the sons your fathers got,
> And God will save the Queen.

He has correctly diagnosed the words in question, which are not so
much a prayer as an expression of hope, 'may the nation flourish',
and he comments accordingly.

A statesman, after describing the delicate balance of the

international situation and indicating the outcome which would be most satisfactory to himself and his audience, ends with the words, 'we must work and we must hope; I fear we must also pray'. It would be naïve to credit him with meaning anything more than this, that the issue depends on factors which may well disappoint our hopes and render our efforts vain.

Miss Dorothy Sayers' fictional detective, Lord Peter Wimsey, speaks of his College: 'We are mortified in nineteenth-century Gothic, lest in our overweening Balliolity we forget God.' It is clear what he means: lest we forget that even Balliol men are subject to the limitations of humanity, lest we be guilty of that self-inflation which the Greeks called *hubris* and which they said provoked the divine jealousy.

These are a few examples where many could be given. They will serve to establish the reality and legitimacy of the use of God-language where no assertion of God's existence is intended.

NON-THEOCENTRIC FORMS OF RELIGION

The term 'religion' covers a great variety of human activities, ranging all the way from public rituals to private prayer and meditation. A particular 'religion' will always be found to include ritual observances, both public and private, a myth and a theology. Linked with these there will generally be found a recommended life-pattern, i.e. a code of conduct which all adherents of the religion are required to observe, and an ideal of character towards which they are encouraged to strive. There will be a pattern of inner life, comprising characteristic attitudes to life and death, to duty and responsibility, to sin and guilt, and probably a doctrine of deliverance from moral and spiritual evil. And there can also be, for chosen souls, a discipline of mind and will whose object is to secure entrance into a higher kind of life – an ascesis leading to a higher knowledge and to some kind of union with the divine.

Rituals; myths and theologies; patterns of moral and social conduct, of inner life and of ascesis – in all these we find great variety, yet all are linked together, and it is the complex system formed by their interactions which we designate by the name 'religion'. Different religions represent different forms and combinations of these elements, but a fully developed religion will contain something of them all.

As there is obscurity concerning the content of the concept of God, so too there is obscurity concerning the part which it plays in the religious complex.

There is a standard view. It is that the concept of God is central and all-important in religion, as God himself is central and all-determining in reality. Man is created to live in close fellowship with God, and religion is the organisation of man's life on that basis. The proclamation of the truth about God is therefore the very heart of religion. The right principles of conduct and self-discipline follow from that; and the rites and symbols exist partly to help in proclaiming the truth and partly to enforce its practical consequences. Thus religion is a coherent system of activities tightly centred upon God.

A different view is held by these who are unwilling to dismiss religion as altogether a waste of time, but who think that the standard view makes metaphysical assertions which cannot be believed. Such people seek the heart of religion rather in the ethic, the ethos, the way of life which it embodies. The life of the soul has many aspects and dimensions and points of crisis, and on a broad interpretation religion may be taken as having to do with all of them. Even the 'delusion' of a personal relationship with God may be recognised as a legitimate stage in growth, though one which should be passed through and left behind. Religion on this view is the great repository of the spiritual experience and wisdom of mankind. Such a view has been held by philosophers like Spinoza and many nineteenth- and twentieth-century idealists, and it is held today by people in the psychological succession of Jung.

There is also a simpler form of the non-standard view, which leaves out the higher flights of the spiritual life and looks only at the every-day fact of morality. Religion is about morality; that is its meaning and there lies its usefulness.

The objection to this latter view is that what we commonly mean by 'religion' is not simply morality, but something more. The difference is clear from both sides. Some types of religion make a point of the contrast between the truly religious and the merely moral man; and on the other hand some people of deep moral commitment would wish to insist that they are not in any way religious. What is the difference? It lies in the ritual observances, the myths and theological formulae, the sacred stories and parables and the ideal characters held up for admiration. Anyone who says that the heart of religion is morality will have to find an explanation for all this. But it is open to him to say that it all serves indirectly to express and enforce moral principles, that the mythologies and the metaphysics, the organisations and the rituals, are part of religion only because they help, or are believed to help, in the formation of character, and that their meaning, properly analysed, will be found to be a symbolic expression of moral ideas.

Thus he could say that God is a personification of the moral will, and his laws and commandments are simply the imperatives of morality. God's judgment on a man is the man's judgment on himself; guilt before God means the unhappiness of an accusing conscience. Hell is a picture of the state of a soul completely divorced from moral principles, alienated from its own best potentialities and from other souls around it, self-enclosed and miserable. Heaven, or the kingdom of God, pictures the society of those who, in a common devotion to duty, live in harmony with themselves and one another. The Christian redemption-story, if we look behind its mythological wrappings, tells us how an exceptional human being can become an embodiment or incarnation of moral worth, and how the influence of such a man can work through long ages for the reintegration and reconciliation of divided and alienated personalities.

A similar analysis could be made of the Buddhist doctrines, showing them to be a metaphysical projection of certain truths about the world and our life in it; the law of cause and effect, the unhappiness that comes from craving, the happiness that grows from detachment, the way in which an inheritance of bad thoughts and habits can be worked out and finally nullified.

So interpreted, the Christian story and the Buddhist story are not in conflict, but are merely different selected aspects of the many-sided truth. It is only when their respective mythologies are taken seriously in the form in which they present themselves that conflict arises, for then they exclude one another. For one who can see behind the mythologies the popular saying is true, that 'all religions are ultimately the same'; that is, not exactly the same, but in close harmony with one another, since all of them are aspects of the same world-wide body of life-wisdom.

A non-standard view on roughly these lines was put forward by Professor R. B. Braithwaite in his Eddington Memorial Lecture entitled *An Empiricist's View of the Nature of Religious Belief*. When this lecture was first published it came to some people as a shock. Yet though Braithwaite's empiricist conception of religion is not one which most religious adherents would openly endorse, there is much in the phenomena of religious life which seems to accord with it. The impartial observer must often be struck by the strange facility with which some people are able to change religions. They go from one form of Christianity to another significantly different form, or they go outside Christianity to Judaism or Islam, or again from these religions to Christianity, often for reasons which have nothing to do with the one belief or the other. It seems often as if the great metaphysical assertions on which the religions are ostensibly built are the last thing to count. A man is received into a new religious community for reasons of personal convenience – marriage or the like – he submits to instruction, makes a profession of faith, and thereafter ceases to assert the doctrines of his former community and begins to talk and live in terms of a different set of formulae. It is hard to suppose that any costing search for ontological truth has been made. To say that the person has decided to exchange one ethical code and one set of edifying stories for another may seem to be a fairer account of what happens.

In a non-standard interpretation of religion such as is here indicated, the word 'God' will often be used and quasi-theological assertions will be made, but in a consciously non-literal sense. How numerous the adherents of the kind of religion may be, no one knows. No one has collected and sifted the evidence which might tell us. Common sense suggests that they may be more numerous than appears at first sight, since they will habitually say and do the same things as the standard-type believers and will thus escape notice; and their number is likely to increase, since the atmosphere of modern thought favours an interpretation on such metaphysically non-committal lines.

For all that, this is not the standard form of religion. The drive and energy of religion as a social and historical force comes from something more positive than this. The rites and myths and theologies were obviously built up in the first place, and are kept up today, by people to whom they have meant and mean something more than a conviction about the principles of morality, important as such a conviction may be. There is a belief in real divine personalities by whom the life of the community is upheld and guided. And there is what is called personal religion, wherein the worshipping soul, not in seeming or in dramatic symbol but in plain reality, traffics with God as self with Self. Two of the most characteristic religious types are the priest, engaged in offering sacrifice and dispensing mysteries, and the devotee, cultivating the so-called interior life in ways which may mean a certain withdrawal from the world's affairs. When types like these come into view, the typically moral man often shows signs of impatience and indignation. He thinks they are wasting time and effort which could have been spent on the improvement of the conditions of human life in this world, the humanising of social relations and so forth. And they themselves have a different conception from this of what they are doing. They think they are having relations with God, each in his own way, and they think that that is of supreme importance in itself. If we accept the view that the essence of religion lies in moral character and conduct, we shall have to regard as irrelevant or eccentric some of the most characteristic forms of religious activity.

OUR PROBLEM REMAINS

My concern in this book is not merely with the God-concept, but with the full standard interpretation of it as the concept of Someone who really exists and acts and reacts with us. This interpretation is by far the most interesting, but it is also the most difficult. With the non-standard usages of 'God' the epistemological problems which have been troubling us would disappear. Where no reality-statement is intended, no knowledge-question arises. But if we are going to take 'God' as an allegedly existing reality, we are back where we were, in the position of having shown that whatever our assertions about him may be, they cannot qualify as knowledge.

What are we to say next? Is there anything more to say, except that reality-statements which fail to qualify as knowledge must not be accepted as true and made a principle to live by?

Perhaps after all there may be something. In view of the numbers of generally intelligent and honest people who adhere to theist beliefs, we may yet to ask whether it is possible to say something more positive about their position. Granted that in being theists they are not knowing reality, can we say what they are in fact doing, and may it be something not unworthy of an intelligent and honest person? Something determines their assent to theist formulations with a confidence comparable with, though manifestly different from, the confidence with which we pronounce when we know. And though their way of thinking is not conformable to what is commonly called reason, they feel no sense of being anti-rational.

Well, there is of course more in life than reason in any sense of that word, and what is different from reason is not necessarily hostile to it. Could that which determines assent to theism be part of this something more, the non-rational but not anti-rational element in life?

It is obvious, indeed, that a certain weighing of reasons does enter into theist thinking, though it is not the decisive factor, and though the reasons which open the way to belief are of a different kind from those which would entitle us to claim knowledge. What then are they? And what is that something else which convinces the theist that he is right to assert what he does assert? What convinces his opponent? What lies at the root of their difference?

To ask these questions is to commit ourselves to an analysis of theist thinking, not in order to judge it by norms extraneous to itself, but in order to find out what its own inherent norms are. It will be found (let me say here by anticipation) that theism is no mere fantasy. It rests upon a structure of argument, which natural theology in its traditional form did much to elucidate, but which we shall have to re-examine from a present-day point of view. And it has links with experience in a variety of ways, which again we must explore. Chapters 5–12 will be devoted to the analysis of the thought-structure of theism. Then Chapters 13–16 will go behind the thought-structure to the real determinants of belief, and will assess the rival claims that such a thought-structure is, and that it is not, worthy of acceptance by a rational person. The whole will amount to an exposure of the inherently dialectical position in which the theist stands in the thought-world of today.

Part II
'AND HEARD GREAT ARGUMENT ABOUT IT AND ABOUT'

5 The Genesis of 'God'

Empirical knowledge is built up by a variety of intellectual operations on the basis of sensory experience. From this given starting-point empirical thinking sets out, and to this it constantly returns to check its findings. God-theory is no part of this structure of empirical knowledge. The concept of God could not even be derived from sense-experience by the processes of empirical thought. Whence then is it derived, and how do people come to a point where they feel justified in asserting the existence of such a being?

God-thinking has a datum of its own, a kind of 'seeing' of God which is its starting-point and stimulus, and to which it constantly returns. The thinking which proceeds on this basis bears a rough analogy to empirical thinking; there is a process of conceptualisation and formation of theories, and a kind of verification through the application of these theories to life. The analogy is, however, a pretty remote one. There is nothing in theology to compare with the directed courses of experimental research with which we are familiar in science, and what I have called the 'verification' of theological theories is lacking in logical rigour and is never conclusive. Theological thinking is really something *sui generis*, whose nature we are now to investigate. And we begin by examining its starting-point, which I call the God-vision.

THE COSMOLOGICAL IDEA

God is not perceived as an object either within or apart from the world. Nor is he analogous to those imperceptible physical entities and processes whose existence is inferred as part of an explanatory theory. In a sense we may be said to 'see' him in the world, though not as a part of the world. We 'see' him in the things and processes of nature, somewhat as one 'sees' a human agent in the things which he makes and the processes which he initiates and controls. The analogy is of course far from perfect. We do not for a moment suppose that God is related to the universe as a man is related to his body and to his handiwork. Nor do we normally profess to read his thoughts and purposes in detail as we often do those of other human beings. All we do is to 'see' his agency in the world around us. It is an intuitive perception which must be looked into more closely. The analysis of it will set us upon a road which will lead at last to the full expansion of natural theology.

Let our first point be, that to say God exists is not so much to say something about God as about the existence of the world. God does not confront us like an object distinguishable from other objects by its quality and structure. We 'see' him at work in the world, which is another way of saying that we 'see' the world as an energising of his. For the world to exist *is* for God to be energising in this way. To put the same thing differently, existence for the world is not self-contained; 'to exist' as applied to the world means 'to be given existence'.

Because we see the world in this way as deriving its being from God, it follows that God himself is never met with, in experience or in pure theory, in isolation, but always in relation to the world, a relation such that he is not there because the world is there, but the world is there only because of him. It is a relation of unilateral dependence. And in the first instance we have no concept of God except as that on whose energising the universe depends. More can be teased out by subsequent reflection. Since God is not seen as depending on something else as the world depends on him, we conceive him as absolute being, absolute existence. And since he is not one of that mosaic of variously differentiated and mutually limiting entities which together make up the world, we think of his being as unaffected by any limitation in relation to any being other than his own. In a word, we think of him as infinite being.

Dr A. M. Farrer in his book *Finite and Infinite* rightly says that the key to natural theology lies neither in the world nor in God, but in the two seen together in this relationship. He calls this schema 'the cosmological idea', and his book is nothing more or less than an explication of it. I cannot follow him in the details of his analysis; my approach is more sceptical than his; but I agree with him as to what it is that we are to study.

We are met on the threshold by the fact of the differences between minds in respect of this idea. Some appear not to be able to grasp it at all, and cannot be brought to see it by any labour of argument or exposition. Others acknowledge it, but as the conclusion of an argument which seems to them to give good grounds for assent. Others again need no argument, but see the point at once, intuitively and unquestioningly. Presumably it is the continuing presence of people like these last which keeps God-belief the living and fascinating and forceful thing that it is.

To say that the point is seen intuitively, however, is not to say that there is nothing in it to analyse. The cosmological idea has implicit in it a number of concepts which it must now be our business to explicate. In doing so we must look for help to the old philosophical discipline of ontology.

BEING AND ACTIVITY

There was a time when a doctrine of being, or ontology, formed the central component of philosophical systems. It is central in the continuing tradition which is called the *philosophia perennis*. Today philosophy has largely turned away from ontology, but theology has not turned away, nor can it do so without cutting off the branch on which it sits. Theology has more in it than ontology; it has a personal aspect. God is not merely That which Is, but He who Is. We shall find this duality of Thatness and He-ness running through the classical arguments of theism and appearing also in religious experience. But the He is the full flowering of the That. The fundamental assertion of theism is not that He Is, but that That which Is is He.

The doctrine of being, which was once central to philosophy and is still central to theology, is essentially a reflection upon three concepts: viz. being, activity and dependence.

What is meant here by 'being'? At any rate not that 'most abstract and general notion of all' which Berkeley found to be 'the most incomprehensible of all', not that 'something in general, which being interpreted proves nothing'. As most philosophers have realised, to be involves being something, involves having a character, a quality or suchness, distinct from that of other beings. In the great tradition of the *philosophia perennis* being is also linked with actuality, activity, energy. What is, energises or acts, and acts in accordance with the kind of being it is: *operari sequitur esse*. And in acting it affects other beings, which again act upon or affect it. They are reciprocally determinative and mutually dependent.

But what, again, is activity?

It is something which is present everywhere in our world, and which we perceive everywhere in our world. We are not surrounded by things existing stolidly side by side and hugging their respective attributes to themselves. They are in constant play and interplay, developing their potentialities in accordance with their own natures and in continual response to one another's influence. There is activity wherever a thing changes its appearance and attributes in accordance with some law of its own nature, or in response to some other thing to which it is its nature to respond in this way, or wherever a thing evokes a responsive change in another thing. Such changes are activities, and the things in and between which they happen are active and interactive. What we call the 'nature' of a thing includes not only the attributes which it can be relied upon to possess, but also the various activities and passivities of which it is capable according to circumstances.

Of the being and activity of inorganic physical things we know nothing except what we perceive or legitimately infer from our perceptions. We can register their sensible attributes, their structures and their process-patterns, and that is all. But we ourselves also are beings and agents, and we know our own being and activity intimately, from within. We know what it feels like to be beings with a definite nature, to be active and passive, determinant and determined, independent and dependent. There is no doubt about the reality of all these conditions, and besides being able to observe them in ourselves and one another, we also experience them inwardly.

From this inward knowledge of being and activity we can construct, by analogy, some conception of forms of being both less and more intense and integrated than our own. We make a guess at the consciousness of many of the animals – though here we have to guard against sentimental tendencies which may lead us to over-humanise the beasts. Some philosophers and some poets have even tried to go further down the scale and attribute some awareness of being, dimly analogous to our own, to inorganic nature; though any attempt to think this out in detail leads to daunting difficulties. In the opposite direction, however, upwards in the scale of being, past the many conceptions of superhuman intelligences with which the history of poetry and mythology and metaphysics is peopled, lies the road which leads to the concept of God.

GOD AS ALL-AGENT

What sets us moving along this road?

The initial stimulus lies in our ability to stand back from the observable world and consider it as a whole. In ordinary life and activity we do not see it thus. We see particular things and persons, forming a plurality of centres of activity all around us, we ourselves being a centre of activity among the rest. But man as a self-conscious subject is able to distinguish and distance himself from the manifold of objects of which he is conscious, to set himself on one side and everything of which he is conscious, whether it be things or persons, on the other side, and to merge them all in the unity of the object-world, the not-self, which in some Indian writings is referred to as 'all this'. And being conscious of himself as a self and a centre of agency, and seeing 'all this' standing over against him and independent of his control, man comes easily to ask 'What agency is behind all this?' Thus the step is taken from recognising the many agencies of which the world is composed to enquiring after an All-Agency at its heart and centre. And since an All-Agency can hardly be supposed to be a less rich and integrated form of being and activity than the richest and most integrated form empirically known to us, namely a self, it easily follows that the All-Agency becomes for us an All-Agent or 'God'.

For an analytical thinker this would at once raise questions – some of the most tiresomely persistent questions of theology. How is the existence of created things related to the existence of God, if they owe their whole being entirely to his energising? How are the agencies of created things related to the all-agency of God? How, in particular, can human beings be the responsible authors of their own actions, if God activates the whole? These are questions which the metaphysician and the systematic theologian cannot avoid. But one who is not a metaphysician or a systematic theologian, or who is not for the moment actively engaged in being either of these, can ignore these questions and stick simply to the point about the All-Agent who activates 'all this.'

The thought-process here is not one of methodical reasoning, like the classical proofs of the existence of God which we shall shortly have to consider. They come later. What comes first is an imaginative outreach. We see the All-Agent in an imaginative flash before we come to build up a structure of argument. Two factors, however, can be identified as giving credibility to the imaginative construction and inclining us to accept it as witnessing to reality. First, the aesthetic appeal of unity and simplicity. In one sense of course the introduction of 'God' complicates things by offering us a new, previously unknown entity which has to be fitted on to what we otherwise know or believe. But on the other hand, to relate all events in the world to a single Agency suggests a unity of pattern and perhaps even of design, which we do not clearly observe but in which we feel drawn to believe. And second, the imaginative projection of 'God' is analogous to the projection which underlies our recognition of other selves in the world. The recognition of other selves is of an importance for our lives which can hardly be exaggerated, and we are innately disposed to hail their presence wherever we recognise it. So too the seeming recognition of a Self manifested in the whole universe and its processes has a compelling power and easily carries conviction. These are factors causative of belief, but of course they are not evidence. The search for genuine reasons belongs to a later stage of sophistication.

GOD AS INFINITE

The imaginative glance reaches out further than we have yet followed it. For the All-Agent must in the nature of the case be unique. Other agents there may be and are in plenty, but they are all derivative from and dependent upon him; none of them are his peers. So he is alone, free and uncircumscribed, or as we say 'infinite'. It is not enough to make him a superhuman being endowed with an intelligence and a power of activity far surpassing ours. That is the concept of a *daimon*, and the gods of polytheism are in fact *daimones*, since, being many, they are finite. God, in the full sense of the term, is infinite both in intelligence and in power. He transcends all finitude, all limitation, all dependence or conditionedness.

Now, the concept of infinite being or infinite activity has a peculiar place among the furniture of our minds, in that it has a more than purely theoretical significance. On the one hand, infinite being or infinite activity is something which we cannot observe or experience in ourselves. It needs an effort of thought and imagination to construct a notion of it, which must in any case be the remotest of approximations to the reality. But on the other hand infinity is not merely something about which we speculate, but something to which in a manner we aspire, and that gives the concept a vividness of meaning and a rootedness in our experience which a merely theoretical construction could not have.

The aspiration takes the form, in the first instance, of an impatience with our limitations, whether they be limitations of material wealth and power, or of physical capacity, or of intellectual or moral or spiritual capacity. Different people feel the shoe pinch in different places according to their character and prevailing interests, but we all feel the pinch in one way or another, and it is a commonplace among moralists and observers of the world that unclouded contentment is, for this reason, always beyond our reach. For it is not a particular limitation that irks us, the transcendence of which would bring satisfaction. If we transcend one limitation only to find others, if we go from a finite to something which is wider but still finite, we are in the end no better off. What we seek is to transcend limitation as such, to become infinite in experience and understanding and wholly free in action. But this we cannot do.

The impossibility is so obvious and so final that in the ordinary business of life we tend to repress the aspiration, pretending to ourselves that we desire, and find satisfaction in, something less. Our intellectual and cultural life is a pursuit of a succession of finite ends, and we profess to find the joy of life in passing on from one task to another, pretending that to travel is better than to arrive, and that final attainment would be a bore. And so it would, if it were the attainment of something finite, and meant being tied down for ever to that. But our real judgment, that no finite can really satisfy, finds expression in that very contention that it is better to travel than to arrive, which means, being interpreted, that it is always better to transcend what can be transcended.

Sometimes we look beyond ourselves, and seek compensation for not being able to be what we would be enjoying the contemplation of it elsewhere. We adopt heroes, whether of legend or of history (which we turn into legend by idealising it). Or we seek in a community what we do not find in individuals, and rejoice to be members of some movement, or nation, or church, which again we tend to idealise out of all reason. For some, this kind of solution may last a life-time without breaking down. The clearer-sighted come to see at last that all their hero-figures and idealised communities are themselves still finite. Vanity of vanities, all is vanity.

So then we seek the infinite, the unconditioned, the absolute in its proper home, which is in God. We form the concept of God as being which is wholly self-sufficient and whose activities amount to nothing less than the creating and sustaining of all that is. God, so conceived, is being in an unqualified sense. He is not something as distinct from something else – that would be a limitation – he *is* without qualification, he is That which Is, *ipsum esse subsistens*. To acknowledge him and contemplate him admiringly is an experience which, for those who know it, takes a central place among all their experiences and activities. To find a way of becoming in some real sense identified with him is the ultimate object of religion.

It should be said at this point (though it should not need saying) that being, activity, infinity and the rest of this group of related terms are not scientific concepts. They arise from pre-scientific reflection upon common experience. By scientific standards they are ill-defined, and they even contain an evaluative element; for activity and energy are generally regarded as good – indeed there is an ancient doctrine that goodness is an inherent and inseparable attribute of being itself. This is not scientific thinking at all, and God is not an object discovered by scientific investigation. He is a speculative construction which is also the hypostatised goal of a deep-seated human aspiration.

THE DANCE AND THE DRAMA

Since these are the sources of the concept of God, the concept always includes something about his relation to the world and to men: to the world, because we arrive at him as the Agency behind all this, and to men, because as infinite and absolute being he has an existential significance for us.

Since God is conceived as an intelligent agent, his action in creating and sustaining the world must be conceived as purposive; and since he acts under no constraint, it is clear that he must create the world to please himself. 'Thou hast created all things, and for thy pleasure they are, and were created.' The mythopoeic imagination, getting to work on this, bodies it forth in more concrete terms. There is for example the sportiveness of God: his creatures are his playthings, his whole action in creating them is one of play. Or there is the divine dance: the whole world dances in joyful homage to God, or in another version he is himself the dancer and the whole world is nothing but the movements of his dance. Both these conceptions, the play and the dance, are common to the Judaeo-

Christian and the Hindu tradition, and are thus no mere local fancies; but they are less to the fore in the western group of religions than in Hinduism, because of the greater ethical emphasis and consequent atmosphere of high seriousness in the western family.

There can be no significant relation between God and men unless there is communication between them; and then everything will depend on what is communicated by God to men and on how they respond to it. It seems to be generally supposed that two main kinds of message come from God, viz. on the one hand moral instructions, with consequential judgments on men's performance in relation to these, and on the other hand expressions of friendly interest and love. The moral instructions show a difference of tone between the eastern and the western group. In India God does not usually speak in terms of command. Krishna for example, in the *Gita*, is rather the supreme heavenly *guru* than the God of the Sinaitic law. But in all the western group of doctrines he appears as absolute legislative authority, absolute commanding will. There is a complexity in men's responses to this terrifying demand, and again a complexity in God's dealings with men in view of their responses. Much is heard of obedience and rebellion, of law and transgression, of guilt and judgment, and the problem of salvation, which is present in all the great religions, wears a much more moralistic aspect in the western group than in India. And in the western group Christianity stands out supreme in the richness of its analysis and the boldness of the action which it ascribes to God. The relation between God and man becomes essentially a dramatic one, a *divina commedia*, and the whole of this world and the next becomes the stage on which this drama is played out. Christianity stands alone among the religions in the power and audacity of its dramatic invention.

What we have just been describing is the growth of a mythology: not one of the multifarious mythologies of polytheism, but the kind of mythology which is proper to a religion whose god really is God. It follows on easily and naturally from the initial imaginative projection which gives us 'God', and it is not to our present purpose to follow it any further into detail than this.

THE VISION OF GOD IN THINGS

These imaginative constructions are not in our thoughts all the time. Like the rest of our ideas and beliefs, they are usually latent in our minds, available for recall and ready to emerge into consciousness at the appropriate stimulus. But where there is firm faith and deep commitment to the belief, it is found that the awareness of God breaks through into consciousness more and more frequently, and may ultimately become habitual if not even continuous. Believers often subject themselves to a discipline of meditation and contemplation to help in bringing this about. And since the All-Agent is not to be thought of out of relation to the world, since to think of him is to think also of that which he activates, an abiding God-awareness inevitably colours one's way of seeing the world. A believer can develop the habit of apperceiving things not merely as the things that they are, but also as manifestations of the divine energy. This awareness can become a vision, suffusing his whole consciousness of things with the manifest presence of God. Such an awareness finds classic expression in many passages of the literature of the great religions.

I am not attributing to the God-seer any special perceptual powers which others do not possess. If he himself is ever tempted to think he has such powers, he is mistaken. The theist has only his senses to inform him about the world, and he has no different sense-data from the non-theist; but he interprets them differently. Like everyone else, he sorts them out and synthesises them so as to present to his consciousness a world of physical things and processes; and the theist's physical things and processes are the same as anyone else's. But they have a further dimension of meaning. The theist sees them not merely as things, possessing certain qualities and attributes, which happen to exist, but as expressions, manifestations, activities of the all-embracing Agency which he believes is at the heart of 'all this'.

VARIATIONS OF THE GOD-VISION

It is clear from the literary and other forms of expression in which the God-vision comes before us that its content can vary. This is not surprising, for the imaginative constructions of the human mind will naturally be influenced to some extent by the cultural environment in which they arise, and perhaps also by ambivalences in the impulses giving rise to them. Especially worthy of notice in the God-vision is the tension between its two outstanding factors: the presentation of the All-Agency as an intelligent purposeful Agent, and the unconditionality and infinity of the Absolute, which seems to forbid us to endow it with quasi-personal characteristics.

In the religions of the western group the personalised God prevails. Their sacred stories all presuppose a God whose mind moves like that of a man, though of course a very wise and very great man. The incomprehensibility of God is acknowledged verbally, but for all that we talk about his nature and his designs as if we were deep in his counsels.

In the Vedanta the personal God is recognised as a legitimate image, valuable for its devotional use, but falling short of the ultimate truth. The God behind all is a God without attributes. But in the welter of diverse cults and theologies which is Hinduism as a whole, the dynamic image of the All-Agent is well to the fore.

In the Mahayana the incomprehensibility seems to have overwhelmed the personality, at least in the more philosophical versions of the teaching. Here too there is a Beyond-All which is the ultimate Source of All, but it is not conceived as a purposeful Agent, and the language in which it is spoken of is impersonal and abstract. The religious desire for a personal attachment to a supernatural power finds satisfaction in a plurality of Buddhas and Bodhisattvas, but the direct personalisation of the Beyond-All, though it does occur, is rare.

About this religious metaphysic of the Far East, however, I know only enough to know that I do not know enough. It is no part of my theme in this book, which is the standard theism of the western religions and especially of Christianity, the one I know best. It is evident that the basic features of the metaphysical vision are worldwide. Everywhere there is the One Source from which the phenomenal world proceeds, everywhere the one Source is unconditioned or absolute, everywhere too the human spirit can seek felicity in some kind of contact with the Infinite. But the details differ widely. It seems clear that the imaginative outreach of the metaphysical vision, deeply as it may influence the thoughts and lives of men, is itself in turn conditioned by the influences of the surrounding culture. As our society shapes us, so we see and so we speak.

THE FEELING OF AWE

A vision such as this, if it possesses the mind, can hardly fail to evoke reactions. Our reactions to this one are complex and paradoxical.

We respond strongly to the power of the All-Agent, so in-exhaustible in the variety of its manifestations and so illimitable in its extent. We view it with wonder and admiration. But this is only possible because it is not brute power, but intelligent power and therefore akin to us. For however staggering may be the difference between the All-Agent and ourselves, as intelligent beings we are still quite truly his kin. As Judaism and Christianity both say, we are created in the image of God; and the realisation of this kinship can bring reassurance, joy and even a kind of exaltation, when in certain moods we feel ourselves drawn into sympathy with the great movement of things. The consciousness of this affinity invests our nature with a peculiar dignity in our own eyes. It does more; it makes us ask whether there can be any kind of communication between God and us. It is well known how fertile the religions have been in thinking of ways in which that might happen.

Yet at the same time there is a remoteness about God, and a mystery, in whose presence we feel diminished and negated. His vast designs are beyond our range, his mode of operation is wholly dark to us, the nature of his inner life and being only distantly conceivable. Hence on our part a mixed reaction, in which sometimes the sense of nearness and kinship prevails, and sometimes the sense of distance and otherness and mystery. When both are present and strongly felt, the complex emotion which results is called religious awe.

In 1917 Rudolph Otto published a book, *Das Heilige* (Engl. tr.: *The Idea of the Holy*), which has been widely accepted as the standard account of this aspect of religious experience. By *heilig* (holy) he means an object capable of arousing awe; that is in fact one possible meaning of the word. He also calls it the numinous, since *numen* in Latin often has this same meaning. He lists the attributes of the numinous, or rather various aspects of the impression which it makes upon us. It is wonderful, paradoxical, mysterious. It is charged with energy, or power, and in that way it is majestic. It fascinates and it terrifies. These are aspects of the human reaction to the perceived presence of the All-Agent.

Otto wrote his book in reaction against a tendency to interpret the concept of God too exclusively in ethical terms. He insists that there is this dynamic substratum, reflecting aspects of 'God' which are far different from those of a supreme moral personality. He did not deny that the ethical aspects are there in 'God' as well, but his book was about the darker side of 'God' and of our reaction to him.

It is particularly in connection with God as seen in nature that this numinous side appears. We believe in, or talk about, the great heavenly Moralist: but in what goes on all around us we see power and mystery.

I shall have more to say in Chapter 10 about Otto's account of the numinous object. Here I am concerned only with his account of the experience of awe, as one in which attraction and repulsion are held in tension together, and with the fact that this is the feeling peculiarly associated with the vision of the All-Agent in things. It is one of the most widely recognised and widely shared of religious experiences, and in Chapter 10 the analysis of the object which arouses it will take us into the depths. For the moment let what has been said suffice.

THE BIRTH OF NATURAL THEOLOGY

I have called the belief in God an imaginative construction, meaning that it arises by intuitive steps with a minimum of explicit reasoning. But that does not mean that there is not a logical structure concealed in it, which analysis might expose to the light of day. And this needs to be done; for an intuition unsupported by evidence or argument may after all be only a fantasy, valuable perhaps as poetry or drama may be valuable, but still not a cognition of reality. It was the work of the traditional natural theology to contend that this was not the case, and that the assertion of God's existence could be shown to follow from a definite line of inference whose starting-point was in the facts of common experience. It was not a scientific inference, but a metaphysical theorem; and if today among philosophers 'metaphysical' is a word of scorn, that does not dispense us from studying seriously the metaphysical thought-structures which have been the backbone of theology.

The work of the new natural theology, to which this present enquiry belongs, must be to re-examine the lines of thought elicited by the older natural theology, and to consider how they stand in the changed intellectual situation of our time.

6 Metaphysical Arguments for the Existence of God

The old natural theology was based on the concepts which we have already found at the heart of theism, viz. being, activity, infinity, absoluteness. With these it tried to construct a line of argument which, starting with propositions about finite things, should end by showing their derivative character and their dependence on an infinite and absolute being which was God. In this and the following chapter we shall see how the argument grew and ramified, and in Chapter 8 we shall examine its cogency.

We shall find that a really cogent argument cannot be constructed with these concepts any more than with those of empirical science. But we shall also find that the endeavour was not fruitless. If natural theology did not discover grounds for belief which could stand up to logical scrutiny, yet at least in the long run it defined the concept of God in ways which have become normative for subsequent discussion, and gave us a vocabulary and a logical map of the ground. We shall not find here the whole of what we are seeking, but we shall find part of it, and be well launched upon our further enquiries.

In so long-lived and well-elaborated a tradition there seems at first sight to be a considerable variety of arguments professing to prove the existence of God; but since they are all embodiments of a small number of principles, there are fewer of them than at first appears. Kant found three, to which I shall add a fourth; and since my attitude to the ontological argument is not quite the same as his, I shall postpone it to the end, and shall begin by examining the argument from contingent being and the argument from design.

THE ARGUMENT FROM CONTINGENT BEING

The argument from contingency goes back to the time when it was thought that philosophical questions could best be formulated as questions about the nature of being, the different kinds of being that there are and the relations between them. Natural theology meant discussing God in these terms, finding the proper place for him in this framework. What kind of a being is he? How does his manner of being differ from the manner of being of things which are not God? How is he related to the other beings and kinds of being which exist? Beings other than God, which are open to our scrutiny as God is not, must be shown to have characteristics from which it follows that they could not exist (as they undoubtedly do) if God did not exist, his existence being the ground or cause of theirs. This thought-process is the heart and core of the old natural theology.

The contingency argument has been stated in a variety of forms, of which the most famous is the argument to God as prime mover, first made clear by Aristotle and developed by St Thomas Aquinas. St Thomas, however, was aware that the argument could be stated in other ways. I shall give it here in the most generalised form I can, so as to make explicit the real kernel of the argument while not distracting the reader with irrelevant details. At the same time I shall try to bring out how many awkward turns the argument has to negotiate before arriving at its goal.

The argument turns on the concept of dependent being. God is presented as that upon which everything that is not God depends both for being what it is and for being (i.e. existing) at all.

It is laid down as a starting-point that there is a relation of dependence in which one being can stand to another being. Some things can only exist because of the existence of other things, and some events can only occur because of the occurrence of other events. In ordinary life we all take this for granted, and apply it to anything that we may happen to be thinking about; we feel that we are getting the hang of things when, and only when, we see how one thing depends on another. There are of course different ways in which one thing can depend upon another. Things can belong together as distinguishable but inseparable parts or aspects of a whole; or, while existing as distinct entities, they can exhibit certain qualities or act in certain ways in response to one another's influence; or one being can owe its very existence to the action of another being. All this is common knowledge.

No being or state of being whose existence depends on the action of another being can exist unless, that, upon which it is dependent, also exists or has existed. Thus if A is dependent upon B, the existence of A is adequate evidence for the existence of B even if we are not able to verify it by observing B; and if B, upon which A depends, itself depends upon C, then the existence of A is adequate evidence for the existence of C. It is by tracing chains of dependence like this that we are able to extend our knowledge of the universe so far beyond our actual sensory experience. It should be added that although for particular purposes, in particular enquiries, we can pick out particular chains of dependence and pursue them with little regard for other factors, on a broader view the whole universe is found to be a single complex of mutually dependent and interacting parts.

Now (says the traditional natural theologian), if there is no break-out from this system of interactions and dependence, if everything has to depend on something else for its ability to be, nothing can actually be at all. Conditional being is not actual being, but only a potentiality, unless the condition on which it depends is actually fulfilled; a world of conditional beings is after all only a world of potentialities, a merely potential world, unless there is something somewhere which unconditionally is, and supplies the condition for other things to be. And since the universe is undoubtedly actual, it follows that there really is a being which is unconditionally actual, and whose actuality actualises the potentiality of all the rest. It must be a being which makes other beings exist without itself requiring to be made to exist, an unconditioned, non-contingent, non-dependent, absolute being.

The foregoing argument can be diversified by taking as a starting-point some particular instance of contingency and arguing from that. So one may begin with the fact that some things are in motion and require a cause for their motion, and conclude to an unmoved first mover. Or one may start from the fact that things come to be and pass away, and argue to an unchanging first cause of all such changes. Or one may argue, from the fact that things in this world possess their various attributes under conditions and limitations, to a primary source of being which is unconditionally and absolutely whatever it is. Or from the fact that a particular essence or nature is endowed with existence at a particular place and time, and only there, one may argue to that whose essence or nature is unconditionally existent. And so on. These apparently different arguments, which at first may bewilder the student of natural theology, are only the one single argument, dressed up with reference to particular instances of conditionality in the hope of making it seem less abstract.

The being which, itself unconditioned, conditions all other beings, is customarily referred to as the first cause. The currency of this phrase is due to the way in which the argument has most commonly been presented. One took a particular causal chain – any causal chain – any series in which A is caused by B, and B by C, and C by D and so on; the conclusion then took the form of saying that such a series could not be actual unless there was a first term which was uncaused, while causing all the rest, in other words a first cause. The phrase is unfortunate because in modern times causality has come to be thought of as a time-relation, so that a causal series is a series of events following one another in time, and a first cause is first in order of time. Hence the question of the existence of God as first cause becomes identified with the question of the coming into existence of the universe at the beginning of a finite period of past time, and theories of cosmogony are thought to have a bearing upon it. But in the heyday of the traditional natural theology causality was not necessarily a time-relation. In particular the causal relation between God and the universe was not so. God, being himself timeless, was the cause of all that is in time by virtue of a timeless act, and the finitude or infinity of the past history of the universe had nothing to do with the question. If the world existed through an infinite past time, it was nevertheless dependent, throughout that infinite past time, on the action of the timelessly existing God for its existence and its duration.

CHARACTERISING THE FIRST CAUSE

I have spoken of the first cause as 'God'. But what is there in common between what we ordinarily mean by that word and the absolute being to which the argument has so far led us? Apparently not much. All we have so far is a list of predicates qualifying the concept of being, all of them very abstract and most of them negative in form. The first cause is non-dependent, non-contingent, unconditioned, absolute. What does this tell us, except that nature is causally dependent on something which is no part of nature, but concerning whose character we can say nothing positive?

Well, classical ontology has rich resources, and from this negative starting-point it can draw out surprising consequences.

(a) The first cause is unconditioned being. But unconditioned entails unlimited, or infinite. Not infinite in spatial extent or in any physical attribute, of course; for we shall see that the first cause cannot be in space, and cannot be a material thing. Infinite being in the present context means being in the fullest sense of the term. The first cause does not 'be' in any qualified sense; it possesses (or rather, is) unqualified reality. It has no attribute which entails limitation of any kind; it has all attributes which do not entail limitation; and it has them without limitation.

The rich terminology of the *philosophia perennis* provides the masters of natural theology with a choice of ways of expressing this conception. St Thomas is associated with the phrase *actus purus*, i.e. not pure activity but pure actuality; there is nothing in the first cause that is merely potential, nothing that the first cause might be but is not. That is one way of expressing the idea. Duns Scotus is content to speak of a being which is actually, and not merely potentially, infinite, and St Anselm means the same by his phrase about that than which no greater can be conceived. Each writer uses the words which fit in best with his favourite thought-pattern, but they all mean the same thing. So does the 'perfect being' of Descartes – a being which has nothing about it to make it less a being, less a reality, than it might be.

(b) But the word 'God' is used as a personal name. Can natural theology say anything in justification of this? It can.

The key concept of the first cause is that it must be in every respect independent, self-contained, self-sufficing. In our world we never meet such an object, but we find in different objects different degrees of approximation to self-sufficiency. It is from this fact of experience that we can feel our way towards a concept of what a completely self-sufficient cause might be like.

No inorganic object can be our model here. Every such object comes to be when the conditions are appropriate and passes away when the conditions are appropriate. While it exists it energises as the conditions allow or determine. It is a dependent or conditioned being throughout its existence, and there is little more to be said. A living being is not so wholly governed by external factors as is an inorganic object. It has, while it lives, a limited but quite real power of self-maintenance and self-enrichment; and it can cause, or partly cause, the coming into existence of others of its kind. There is a hint of self-containedness and self-sufficiency here, the more so as we move towards the more highly organised types of animal life. Yet even man, the most flexible and self-determining of all animals, is still dependent ultimately upon physical conditions which determine his birth and his death and limit his opportunities for action. There is no helpful analogy here on which to conceive the first cause.

The traditional natural theology seeks one in a 'spiritual' or immaterial being. But what is that?

In ordinary life we often speak of a man's mind, or soul, or personality, in distinction from and without reference to his body. We have a copious vocabulary for this purpose. Now, there is a long tradition of teaching to the effect that a human personality can exist and function in separation from, and after the death of, the body. To think that is to treat it as an entity in itself, not merely distinguishable from the body for purposes of discourse, but essentially distinct from it. It has traditionally been held that it must be such as to occupy no space, unextended, uncompounded and so immaterial.

But if a disembodied human soul or spirit is agreed to be conceivable, so also is a spiritual being which never unites with a body, and, being free from the limitations necessarily involved in such a union, is by its nature a more powerful intelligence and a freer and more independent agent than man. Such are the gods and daemons of polytheism and the angels of monotheism. But even the gods of polytheism were still conceived as having an origin in something beyond themselves, something truly unoriginated and unconditioned. Polytheists have often been content to leave the nature of this Ultimate shrouded in mystery; but to the more philosophical among them, and to monotheist thinkers, it has seemed evident that such a being should also be conceived as an intelligent agent, the ultimate originating source of all agency and all existence.

Of course he must be unique. He cannot be merely an intelligence among intelligences, not even the greatest of them all, if his greatness is still a finite greatness. For we have seen that his being is infinite, unqualified, unlimited being. So likewise must his attributes be. He must be infinite intelligence, infinite knowledge and wisdom, infinite breadth of design; that is to say, there is nothing of which he is ignorant, no value which he cannot weigh, no complexity of which he is not master. Every kind of intellectual competence which we have sometimes, in a degree, he has timelessly and absolutely. As Aristotle puts it: 'If God is always in the same good state as we are sometimes, it is a wonderful thing; and if more so, still more wonderful; but such is the case.'

Here is a first cause which can hold our interest, and the belief in which can give a sense of meaning to our lives. Even Aristotle, who was no religious enthusiast, saw this well enough. In the next chapter I shall explicate some of the ways in which belief in God makes life seem meaningful. Before that, however, let us look for a moment at the next great argument of natural theology, the argument from design, which confirms the conclusion so far arrived at and correlates it with specific evidences in experience.

THE ARGUMENT FROM DESIGN

The argument from contigency is lengthy; it is expressed in abstract metaphysical terms; and in its course it makes many assumptions and jumps many difficulties. The argument from design is simple; it does not work with abstract concepts like being, contingency or even causality, but with the well-known and familiar concept of purpose; and it leads not to a non-contingent first cause, leaving us to work out afterwards what that may be, but directly to an intelligent divine agent. We need not therefore be surprised that it has been held to be the most consistently popular of all the arguments for the existence of God.

The evidence which it offers for the existence of God as an intelligent agent is the presence of clear traces of purposive contrivance in the universe.

What are the evidences of purposive activity? What phenomena must we observe if we are to feel justified in applying this concept?

The characteristic feature of a purposive process is the con-vergence of a variety of factors, different from and in a degree independent of one another, which interact and combine so as to produce a result which has a unity of structure and function. Where we find such a convergence, we tend to see it as the carrying out of a purpose, and therefore suppose that there exists a purposive agent whose action the process is.

It is easy to pick out structures and processes in nature which, on a first view, display these characteristics. It is especially easy where the end-result, which appears to us as the purpose of the process, is somehow related to our own concerns and purposes. That is how the departmental gods of polytheism are discovered and their provinces assigned. For example, the annual flooding of the Nile, which makes what would otherwise be a desert into a fertile land and a home for a nation, is a clear case. It is obvious that there is a Nile god whose beneficent work this is.

The people who created polytheism were intelligent and imaginative people, who in their own language were talking about realities. They were, however, not imaginative enough. They could single out particular groups of phenomena and construct a divine personality behind each, but they did not take in the broad sweep of nature as a whole. When one sees how the behaviour of rivers, including the Nile, results from a wide range of influences which are essentially the same all over the world, it ceases to be convincing to postulate a god for the Nile by itself. That does not mean that there is no divine purpose behind the behaviour of the Nile; but it means that there must be a power whose purpose embraces the whole river system of the world, with the geological, meteorological and other conditions which make it possible. We shall then say that this power, while ordaining that there shall be rains and springs and rivers to water the earth and make it fruitful, incorporated in his world plan those factors which give rise to the special instance of the Nile and its meaning for Egypt. It will then not be long before all the purpose characteristic of the departmental gods come to be seen as details in the all-comprehending purpose of the One God.

The step to natural theology is taken when, instead of simply seeing things and processes as God's work and the execution of his purposes, we try to prove that they are so. It is the step from intuitive vision to analytical reasoning.

There is only one argument which can do the necessary work. To show that a phenomenon is the result of a superhuman purposive agency we must show that it cannot be explained in any other way; and to do that we must show that the various natural factors involved, taken simply as what they are in themselves, cannot account for the unity of structure and function which in fact emerges from their interaction. For example, when a human agent, in pursuit of his purpose, puts together the materials which make a building, or organises pen, ink and paper into the MS. of a book, he gives to his tools a progressive pattern of action, and to his materials a final unity of structure, of which they by themselves are not capable. It is not in the nature of a pen to rise up and write; it needs a man to make it do so, and the man acts so because he has a purpose. Natural theology, in so far as it thinks in terms of purposes, argues on this analogy. It says that there are in nature instances of a patterned unity of action and structure, which cannot be accounted for in terms of the physical factors involved, taken simply as what they are in themselves. The unity, the order must come from another source acting upon the physical factors; and the only order-imparting agent which we know is that of which we ourselves are an instance, viz. intelligence conceiving and executing purposes. Such is the traditional argument from design.

The signs of a purposive divine agency are sought sometimes in the order of the universe as a whole, and sometimes in particular phenomena within it.

One argument starts from the fact that there is a universe or world order (*kosmos*) at all. For, it says, the elements of which the universe is composed have not in themselves the capacity to arrange themselves and maintain themselves in a regular order such as we actually find. Since the order is there, we must conclude that there is a reason why it is there; and the production of order in what would else be disorderly is a characteristic of purposive activity. This is the thought which finds expression in many creation myths, according to which there was once a chaos, but then a divine agent stepped in and imposed order on it. What the myths present as a temporal sequence (what was at first – what came later) is presented in the theological argument as a logical progression (what existence might have been – what in fact it is). In both modes, God as giver of order mediates the transition.

An argument for divine purposivity is often developed from the phenomena of life, and many facts are brought in evidence.

To begin with, there is the bodily structure and functioning of living organisms, the co-ordination of their different organs so as to serve the life of the whole, their capacity for growth, for self-adjustment and recovery of balance after disturbance or injury, and for reproduction.

Then there are their behaviour-patterns, directed so variously and so efficiently towards obtaining food, shelter, safety, a mate, or the safety of their young; behaviour-patterns which can include complex processes like nest-building and even the organisation of complex social systems. There is sometimes a flexibility of response to stimuli, a capacity to investigate and to learn from experience.

There is also the striking way in which some animals are adapted, in bodily structure and capacity and also in instinctive equipment, to the physical environment which is theirs.

And beyond all this there is the story of evolution, the development of living forms from simple beginnings, past various false starts and unsuccessful ventures, towards a richness of consciousness and a co-ordination of responses which is at its highest, so far at least as this planet is concerned, in man.

In all these phenomena we are invited to see evidences of purpose at work, and since the animals involved cannot themselves be supposed to have the power either to conceive these purposes or to execute them, the facts point directly to God.

Analogous to the argument from evolution, but resting on a narrower base, is the argument from the course of history. The concept of progress in history, and of the historical record as a record of progress, has become very familiar to us in modern times. It dominates and pervades most teaching and writing which deals with events on a large time-scale. At particular times and places, undeniably, there have been failures and retrogressions; but (it is said) one has already to take a wider view to see that these are mere passing episodes in the story of human advance. Now, of course we know that all human beings have purposes. The dynamic of history is in the purposes of human agents or of human collectivities, which spur them on to act as they do and so bring about the results which they do. On the small scale, the events of history are accounted for (apart from what is due to the working of natural forces) by the purposes of the human agents engaged in it. But (it can be argued) if we take a wide enough view we become aware of a grand design which transcends the purposes entertained by the human agents through whom it is wrought out. Men and nations work better than they intend, better than they know. And the explanation of this can only be that they are instruments in the service of a more comprehensive purpose than any of their own, in fact of God's purpose.

One thing must be said about the argument from design in all its possible forms. Even if it is unobjectionable as an argument, it cannot by itself sustain the whole weight of religious theism; for it only proves a purposeful controller of the world, whereas the religious concept of God is that of a creator. In fact, the traditional natural theology never pretended that the argument from design was the sole or even the principal reason for believing in the existence of God. Popular as it might be, and useful sometimes in turning the mind in the direction of theological enquiry, it was only an introduction to, or an amplification of, the really decisive argument, the argument which found the inescapable evidence of God in the heart of all contingent being. And although the ordinary believer in God is no philosopher, there is something here, I believe, which answers to the movement of his thought. The ideas contained in the argument from design do play a part in forming and sustaining religious belief, but it is a subordinate part, and what really determines the mind to belief is something more deeply rooted than this. Whether the argument from contingency itself adequately represents this deeper thing, is a question about which there will be more to be said. In any case there is yet another type of argument which demands consideration.

THE ARGUMENT FROM INTELLIGIBILITY

There is yet another argument of a metaphysical character, based not on the concept of being but on that of intelligibility. From Plato ('the wholly real is wholly knowable') down to Hegel ('the real is the rational and the rational is the real') and Bradley ('the real is that which satisfies the demands of the intellect') there runs a line of doctrine which makes the connaturality of thought and being a first principle and uses it as an instrument for the discovery of the Ultimate. Especially worthy of our notice is the form which this doctrine took in nineteenth- and twentieth-century idealism; for philosophers and theologians belonging to that school or influenced by it argued the case for theism on just this ground, that it gives the most intellectually satisfying and therefore the truest account of things that we can conceive.

Behind it there is a theory of knowledge with a strong intellectualist slant. Things exist, and are what they are, whether we know about them or not. Our knowledge of them may not be profound, but if we are to know them at all we must know them as they are, not as we should like to think they were. That is elementary common sense. And yet the mind in knowing is active: seeking, combining, discriminating, judging, inferring. It does these things in order to get beyond mere impressions to facts, and beyond mere facts to an explanation of them. We explain a particular fact by showing that it is part of a system of relations which, taken all together, require that it should be as it is. We explain a complex body of facts by exhibiting a principle in their mutual relations, by virtue of which they constitute a system. When we have arrived at an explanation of a body of facts, and only then, we consider ourselves to have got to the bottom of it, to know the truth of it, to understand it as it really is. Thus the discovery of a principle of explanation is regarded as the disclosure of a reality-structure.

True, an explanation can cover the facts as known at a given time and be discarded later because of fresh facts which it does not cover. But it would be rash to draw sceptical conclusions from this. When an accepted explanation is shown to be unworkable we give ourselves no rest until we find a better one to take its place; and in science we expect, and generally find, that the new explanation includes the superseded one as an approximation to the truth. The ultimate explanation, which is also the ultimate truth about reality, is something which we can never expect to attain in detail, and yet can never cease to pursue; and implicit in this pursuit is our obstinate trust that by satisfying our desire for an explanation of things we are following a thread which leads to reality.

By putting the demand for an explanation in place of the demand for a cause, one could translate the argument from contingency into these terms on something like the following lines: for every fact there must be an explanation, and a fact is explained by being shown as part of a system. For a full and complete explanation the system in question would have to be nothing less than the whole universe. But more is required; for an explanation may be complete in its own terms and may yet leave some kinds of question unanswered, or may give rise to fresh questions with which it itself cannot deal. Then we have to look beyond it for a more powerful principle of explanation. Unless all explanation is to remain partial and inconclusive, there must be a principle of explanation which does not leave questions unanswered or raise fresh questions beyond itself, a principle which brings all questioning to an end, leaving the mind to repose in the achieved truth. Only then can the demands of the intellect be satisfied and the nature of reality known.

What is this wholly satisfactory principle of explanation? Not (so runs the argument) the natural-science model of events taking place in accordance with a law; for in that system it remains unexplained why the laws should be what they are, or why these particular events should occur under them. Better is the analogy of an organic whole, wherein the detailed incidents and the prevailing laws are seen to be merely different aspects of the purposivity of the whole. But a greater wealth of internal differentiation and at the same time a more intimate unity and interpenetration of the different aspects is found in a self, or personality, which asserts and consciously enjoys its unity amid all the diversity of its contents. A human selfhood moreover expresses itself by throwing out imaginative inventions and practical projects which it executes *ad extra*. Here is a model which we thoroughly understand, because it is our own nature. Here is the principle of explanation of which we have been in search. Only we must add that whereas man, being finite, grows and enriches himself by his inventions and outward actions, God, who is in himself complete and self-sufficing, expresses or manifests what he timelessly is by his creation of the temporal world.

And then, of course, those facts of experience on which the argument from design is based fit in easily to illustrate and confirm our conclusion.

THE STRANGE CASE OF THE ONTOLOGICAL ARGUMENT

The intelligible coherence of the theist world-picture can be apprehended intuitively, without being spelled out in abstract analyses and reasonings. One who enjoys the God-vision described above in Chapter 5 may apprehend it in this way without consciously thinking it out. In that case the apprehended intelligibility and coherence will become simply a special quality in the God-vision itself, which will appear to such a person as inherently authoritative and obviously true. It will seem to him that one has only to think of God to see immediately that he is real and the centre of all reality.

The possibility of this intuitive conviction may serve to explain the strange history of the ontological argument.

'By "God" we mean a being which lacks nothing that can be conceived as an enrichment of its nature, the greatest (or richest) being that can be conceived, the most perfectly endowed of beings. Now, such a being cannot lack existence, because if it did, it would not in fact be the greatest or richest or most perfectly endowed being that can be or be conceived. A being otherwise identical with it, but possessing also existence, would be the real greatest, richest, most perfect of beings. Hence the greatest or richest or most perfect of beings, i.e. God, must necessarily be a being which exists.' Somehow thus may be explicated the argument which is advanced in different formal terms by St Anselm and by Descartes, and is known as the ontological argument.

It is refuted simply pointing out that existence is not a quality of things which could count as an enrichment or perfection of their nature. That is not how the term 'existence' works at all. To say that a being exists is to say nothing about its nature, about how it could be defined or described; it is to say that we are constrained to accord it recognition and to take account of it in our serious (as distinct from fanciful) thinking. You cannot establish this constraint merely by defining the being in a certain way. The ontological argument rests on an elementary philosophical blunder, and that is all that need be said about it.

But is it? Why then is the argument continually remembered in spite of its repeated refutations? Why does it continue to fascinate even some who have clearly seen through it as it is commonly stated? Surely because they sense behind it the presence of an insight which the argument fails to express accurately, an insight quite other than the flimsy trick which the argument overtly presents.

Anselm in the preface to the *Proslogion* tells us what launched him upon the enquiry which led to the creation of the argument. He had already written the *Monologion,* in which he had set forth the grounds for belief in God on traditional lines derived from Augustine and ultimately from Plato. But he was not satisfied. The arguments were too numerous, too complex and involved. He wanted to find one simple argument which would do all the work by itself. After much perplexity he finally saw – or thought he saw – a way of conceiving God which was such that you had only to think of him to see straight away that he must be real. Anselm's attempt to formulate his discovery is the argument given in the *Proslogion,* and we are bound to say that if that is really what he saw, his discovery was a mare's nest. But in view of what we know of Anselm's intellectual quality, and of the thrill which it is still possible to feel when reading or remembering what he writes, it is tempting to conclude that what he has really done for himself, and indirectly for us, is to attempt to articulate the experience of finding that to think of God as the richest object that can engage the intellect is to see in a flash that this is Reality.

This interpretation would explain and partly justify the strange rehabilitation which the ontological argument underwent at the hands of Hegel and other philosophers and theologians influenced by him. These writers did not try to reinstate the Anselmian or the Cartesian formulation; they knew that these are beyond saving. But they looked through these formulations to the basic intuition, and they realised that it concealed within itself the assumption that human thought can explore the nature of things to its ultimate source. This intellectual titanism was a declared principle in their own philosophy. Accordingly they interpreted Anselm's argument as an imperfect attempt to assert their own fundamental principle. C. C. J. Webb, in editing a translation of the *Proslogion*, put the point succinctly: 'The ontological argument of Anselm is, if properly explained, sound, supposing we assume that *thought is the criterion of reality*; or rather, it *is* just the assertion that thought is this criterion; . . . that therefore that is the *most real* which is *the most satisfactory to thought*.'

Historically this is not correct; the ontological argument does not argue from the principle that thought is the criterion of reality, still less is it a mere assertion of that principle. The readiness of some philosophers since Hegel's time to pretend that it is, is an interesting case in the psychology of self-deception. But they evidently felt in Anselm's writing the presence of something which did not come to utterance in the overt argument, and they diagnosed it, correctly as I incline to think, as the principle 'thought the criterion of reality' working unconsciously on the deeper level of mind.

7 Meaningfulness and Mystery

The argument from design does not suffice by itself to bring us to a God who is really the Ultimate. Only some form of the argument from contingency does so, and that argument, which is certainly abstract, may appear remote and empty if seen in isolation.

History, however, does not present it to us in isolation, but as part of a body of metaphysical doctrine. Attached to it are riders, or theorems consequential upon it, and we shall see that these are of two kinds. One group, of positive import, explores consequences which bring God into an intelligible relation with human life and experience, so making theism easier to understand and accept. The other group, by exposing the inherent difficulties of conceiving God, has the opposite effect. It is only fair to examine both these sets of consequences before forming a conclusion as to the merits of the theist argument.

THE ETHOS AND ETHIC OF THEISM

We are bidden to conceive God as an intelligent agent; and though mind and will in God must be different from mind and will as we know them in ourselves, yet, if words are to have any meaning at all, we feel entitled to draw out conclusions from the analogy. The first and fundamental one is that an intelligent agent entails an intelligible work. The universe therefore, being God's work, is essentially intelligible.

That does not mean that it may not contain patches of genuine disorder or random chaos; for an intelligible design might call for the presence within it of real unintelligibilities as incidents in the wider whole. In that case the random bits would be intelligible after all, in the formal sense that it was possible to understand why they were there, though they would have no intelligible structure in themselves. Again, to say that the universe is essentially intelligible does not mean that everything in it is intelligible to us. What is intelligible in itself is not necessarily so to the human mind, which works under difficulties. In view of these qualifications, what remains of the statement that the universe is essentially intelligible? No hard information at all, but an invitation to take a certain attitude to things, an encouragement to enquire boldly in the faith that if we seek order and intelligibility in things we are likely sooner or later to find it.

In mediaeval scholasticism it was accepted doctrine that every being (*ens*) is in some degree true (*verum*) and good (*bonum*). By saying that every being is true they meant that there is something in it for the intellect to apprehend, some degree of intelligible order. By saying that *ens* is good they meant that there is something in it which an intelligent observer can appreciate and find in some degree satisfying. The one entails the other, in fact, since where an intelligent mind apprehends order, it also appreciates or enjoys it. This doctrine of the inherent truth and goodness of being was not invented by the scholastics. Its roots are in Platonism. During many centuries it seems to have been regarded as a known truth about the nature of being as such. That was a mistake; the *verum – bonum* doctrine cannot be known simply by studying the nature of being, but only, if at all, as a conclusion from an already accepted theism, in the manner in which I am presenting it here. It is a doctrine not so much of the nature of things as of the relation between things and the human mind and will. This world, being God's world, is a world fit for intelligent beings to live and exercise their powers in.

One can go further. God has made things, i.e. caused them to exist, and caused them to be such as they are. We can therefore say that their natures are an articulate expression of his thought about them and his will for them. Since he has made them like this, he means them to be like this, to act and function and develop as they do. And this has interesting consequences when we come to beings like ourselves, who have a consciousness of their own identity and nature and an ideal of what they would like to be or to become. We must take it that such beings have these ideals because God means that they should have them; and in pursuing their ideals they can be regarded as conforming to God's will for them. And so a kind of personal relationship is established between him and them.

Here I must insert a caution. Most people in the English-speaking world know the phrase 'doing the will of God' in a Jewish or

Christian context. In that context the phrase connotes (or is very widely taken to connote) a set of commands and prohibitions, revealed to men by God and backed up by a system of rewards and punishments. Doing the will of God then means doing as one has been told, in a spirit of docility and obedience. It is evident that such a conception can have no place in our present enquiry. In our language 'the will of God for us' is simply those ideals and principles which it lies in our God-given nature to form and to pursue. We need not verbalise them as commands and prohibitions at all. If we do, as the ancient Greeks as well as the Jews sometimes did, the voice which promulgates them will be the voice of reason in us, and it will be God's voice only in the sense that reason in man is a reflection of the creative intelligence which is God. So much so that what may be called obedience to God's law may equally well be described as the imitation of God; and that is the ordinary way of regarding it in the Platonic tradition. The Jew and the Christian know this conception too, of course.

It is a principle recognised both by the eudaemonist philosophers and by Kant, that intelligent beings regard intelligence with respect wherever they find it, in themselves and in one another. We respect the integrity of our own nature, including not only the mind but the body which is its instrument. We shrink from unnecessary mutilation of the body, and we disapprove of actions which employ bodily or mental capacities in ways which frustrate what we think are their proper functions. We also respect the works of intelligent beings – inanimate objects in which they have exercised their skills and expressed something of their mind. Human beings in a rational frame of mind do not wantonly destroy or deface the works of other human beings, their houses and orchards, paintings and buildings, writings, cultural habits and the like. This respect for intelligence and its expressions accounts for a great deal in the complex fabric of our *mores*, and it is not surprising that philosophers have often singled it out and made it the basis of moral theories, which are essentially attempts to rationalise our *mores* by detecting a principle at work in them.

Now, if this principle of respect for intelligence and its expressions is firmly rooted in us, and if we also believe in the existence of God and in his nature as supreme intelligence, we naturally assume towards him an attitude of supreme respect, an attitude which goes beyond what we generally call respect and verges on worship, an attitude of unqualified admiration, homage and loyalty. Our cultivation of rationality in ourselves becomes a conscious imitation of God in loyalty to his purpose for us. Our respect for other intelligent beings becomes a respect for his image in them. The world itself, especially where living creatures are concerned, we regard not as a free field for exploitation, but we look for, and seem to ourselves to discern in it, a balance which must be respected. We feel not merely imprudence, but guilt, in the waste or destruction of natural resources, the unnecessary destruction of animal species and the wanton destruction of natural beauty. All this puts man into a genuinely personal relation with God, not directly, but through man's reading of the world-order.

Such views are encouraged by the revealed religions, but they do not require any belief in a revelation for their support. They arise quite naturally from the basic theism which natural theology formulates. There have even been philosophical systems (Platonism, Stoicism) which recognised and incorporated this view of things.

If man is thus brought into a personal relationship with God, we can go yet further and describe it as a dramatic relationship. For man is free to open his mind to these consequences of theist belief, or to refuse to see them, or even to go against them in practice. Here then we have two wills, God's and man's, which may converge, or diverge, or even conflict; and the relation between them can change from positive to negative or again from negative to positive. But where we have this, we have a dramatic situation, the kind of situation which is the substance of the most serious types of drama.

If we further hold that the position which man takes up towards God is of importance for man's ultimate destiny, this dramatic situation in which man stands becomes charged with infinite significance. It becomes appropriate to ask whether God can and does make some further appeal to man, besides that which is contained in the very fact of creation, so as to induce him to see wisdom. It becomes appropriate to enquire whether there has been any special revelation from God to man. It is no part of natural theology to pursue that question, but it is legitimate to indicate how natural theology, if pressed hard, can bring us to the point where the question arises. The revealed religions themselves sometimes urge this upon us. We are familiar with a line of argument among Catholic apologists according to which, while only the gift of faith can enable us to recognise God's revelation in Christ, natural reason can bring us to the point where we are bound to ask whether there is such a revelation, and to start looking for it. A not dissimilar thought is implicit in the Quran, in those passages which appeal to the manifest 'signs' of himself with which God has filled his creation. These signs are visible to all men, not only to believers, and they ought to be enough to turn all men into believers, i.e. believers in the existence of One God who is the Judge of men, and so make them able and ready to recognise the significance of the Prophet when he appears among them.

MENS CREATRIX?

The foregoing results were obtained by pressing hard the implications of the concept of God as a personal being. But he is also unconditioned, absolute, infinite being, infinite in all his attributes. What happens when we take this side of the matter seriously?

We find ourselves receiving a sharp reminder that in speaking of the mind and will of God we are using familiar words for something whose nature is far different from anything with which we are familiar. We find that personality, when pushed into the absolute, loses most of the attributes which we know in our experience of it, and displays others of which our experience gives only the most tenuous hint, or none at all.

To begin with, here is an intelligent personality existing and functioning without a physical body. A century or two ago it was common usage to refer to him as the Supreme or Eternal Mind. But we know no empirical instance of a mind, eternal or not, existing as an entity in itself. Intellectual processes, so far as we can clearly see, occur only in conjunction with a nervous system of a particular structure and complexity, and derive their content and direction from the perceptions and drives of the organism to which this nervous system belongs. To assert the existence of God is to assert the existence of a kind of personality which never had a body, which did not come into existence and develop its content and character in the way that all personalities in our experience do. It would be hazardous to say that this is impossible, but we ought not to disguise from ourselves what a large assumption it is.

This bodiless personality is supposed to be the cause of the existence of the material world. All minds empirically known to us exist in the material world and depend upon it for their ability to function at all; but this one causes the universe itself to exist. This is a kind of causality for which we know no model. Neither the causality-concepts of natural science nor those of the social sciences are any help here. True, we can say one thing about the divine causation: being the action of an intelligence, it will presumably be purposive, and we know about purposive causation from our own experience of it. But what operation is it which God is alleged purposefully to perform? We have no idea. Minds as we know them create nothing. They merely process material received by way of sensation from the surrounding physical world, and they do so to suit the needs of an organism living in that world. But the divine mind is supposed to invent, without stimulus or raw material or guiding need, the entire universe which it brings (no one knows how) into existence. It will be said that he invents it and provides it, not out of sheer nothing (whatever mythology may say), but out of the inexhaustible store of being which he has in his own nature. Perhaps; but minds as we know them do not have such a store of being within themselves. They are merely crystallisations in the mode of consciousness of some aspects of the great sea of being which laps around them.

Then too we have here a personal agent whose products are not only things, but include other personal agents, who have their own conscious existence distinct from his, and a degree of independence in thought and action which allows them to ignore him or even turn against him, as we see they frequently do. How are we to conceive this creation of beings who, while depending absolutely upon their creating cause for their very existence, are yet able to assert themselves so independently of him? True, we may find a certain analogy in the relation between the mind of a dramatist or a novelist and the characters whom he 'creates'. While up to a point these characters express something in the mind and character and experience of their author, yet it is a known fact that as they develop in the course of a work or a series of works they take on an independent character of their own, which their author observes and records, but can violate or ignore only at his peril. The author is not personally responsible for what his characters do, though he is of course responsible for writing and publishing the book which contains them. But after all the human author does not give his characters a distinct substantial existence, as God does with his; and here, as always, before the alleged fact of creation our power of conception breaks down.

LOOKING BEYOND FINITUDE

A different kind of problem arises when we ask ourselves what kind of consciousness, what kind of selfhood is to be attributed to God. We know something of our own selfhood from inner experience; and as we conceive other selves by imputing to them an inner life analogous to our own, so we naturally think at first that we can form a concept of God – of his thoughts and feelings and purposes. But of course the analogy will be less close between ourselves and God than it is between one human being and another. God being as he is, bodiless and subject to no limitation or restraint, thinking and feeling and willing must be very different indeed in him from what they are in us.

For example, personality entails knowledge and will. Knowledge in our experience comes by way of sense-perception and acquaints the knower with an objective world of which he is himself a part. Will arises by way of stimuli which evoke a conscious need and so lead to the formulation of ends and means. But God is no part of the universe. He is the cause of its existence; it depends totally upon him and he depends upon nothing at all. He has no body, no sensations, is not provoked to action by external stimuli, has no needs which he might seek to satisfy. In this quite fundamental respect, what it is like to be God is unlike anything we can know.

More particularly, our knowledge of things depends upon the things themselves as existing and affecting us. God's knowledge does not depend upon things; it is perhaps more like what we ourselves possess in the case of things which we make – the thing is known as a project before it is given existence, and is known as existing in and with the act of giving it existence. But of course our making is always a rearrangement of materials which we did not make, but found or received; whereas God's is wholly from within his own being. Further, since he does not obtain information by way of sensation, in bits and pieces, as we do, he has none of the work to do that we have in synthesising and interpreting our data. No discursive scrutiny, no questioning or answering, no asking or learning; no abstract concepts, no abstract general propositions, no inferences, no theories, no linguistic symbols, but one totally comprehensive and totally concrete apprehension. Since God is not subject to change, his knowledge does not grow or undergo any enrichment with the passage of time and events, but embraces all the time in a timeless apperception. And whereas our intellectual life swings between unity and plurality, finding satisfaction in neither alone, yet wondering helplessly why and how they coexist, in God's intellect they must rest in a luminous interpenetration.

Again, God's actions do not arise in response to any pre-existing situation, since the coming into existence of any situation is itself his own act. He does not formulate an end and then deliberate about means, nor does he choose between competing desires and rival purposes, but conceives and creates his objects in total harmony and in total detail, seeing all and willing all in one sovereign act. He never has to adjust his plans to fresh circumstances, but is always master of fact and of process. Nor can he be said to foresee or foreknow future events, because no events are future to him. The execution of his purpose is manifested in time as a process of events, but the volition, as it is within his own being, is timeless and all-inclusive.

In the *philosophia perennis* 'will' often means love, and God must be thought of as having a love or complaisance towards his universe. But he is also held to be displeased at some things in it, and displeasure as we know it is a matter of finitude and frustration, which are not to be attributed to God. He must somehow be displeased without being diminished or hurt; his frustration and disappointment must be somehow elements in a total experience which is one of unqualified joy. It is easier to say this than to understand it.

A further point is perhaps less immediately obvious. All human consciousness known to us is the consciousness of living human beings, and includes a partly articulate, partly unanalysed, mass of bodily sensation. The structure of our consciousness is built up around this as a kind of centre. Even our perception of lengths and distances is not purely visual but includes a strong element of kinetic sensation as well. And our visual field is built outwards from a kind of window through which we look out upon the world; the seeing subject appears to himself to be at a point closely related to the eyes, and so to the head, and so to the body as a whole. Not that he sees himself as being at that point, but he looks out upon the world as if from that point. In consequence all sensible objects are perceived or imagined from one only of an infinite number of possible points of view. This is an element of finitude which can find no parallel in God. To him we can attribute no central body-consciousness, no outward view upon things as through a window, no limitation to one point of view. In a word, we cannot credit him with a field of consciousness in the least degree resembling our own, nor can we conceive what, in his consciousness, could be the relation between subject and object. What then can we mean, at the end of the day, by speaking of him as seeing or knowing things at all?

Furthermore, a distinction is to be drawn between God's awareness of his creatures and his awareness of his own being, and we may ask what kind of awareness this latter is supposed to be. We human beings have a kind of self-awareness and self-enjoyment, but it is very largely if not entirely an awareness of our bodily selves; or if not, it is an awareness of our mental activities in relation to external objects, our perceptions and thoughts and feelings about them, and not a conscious possession and enjoyment of our own being, whatever that may mean. What in fact *is* the inner being or content of our mind, as distinct from the content of its object-consciousness? Shall we say with the Augustinians that it is the *memoria* as distinct from the *intellectus*? But the *memoria* is a storehouse of material which is only potentially in consciousness, and nothing like that is to be ascribed to God. What can be the character of the inner experience of a being who does not simply know objects which he finds already there, nor even objects which he conceives and creates as distinct from himself, but has himself an inward reality from which theirs is derived, but which immensely exceeds anything of theirs, and which is inherently transparent and luminous to himself?

These conclusions may startle, but they are not a confession of total ignorance. If we deny many things of God, things which are of the very substance of our own life and experience, it is because we predicate other things of him, and these things too are not meaningless to us. We argued in the previous chapter that it is possible to form a concept of God as a centre of activity, self-contained, free, infinite in all attributes and operations. All that we have been doing just now is to work out in detail what such a concept would have to be. All that is finite, conditioned, passive in our own experience and activity has been thought away from it, but we are not left with nothing. For in fact a kind of dissociation of these experiences from finitude is implicit in our experience. It lies in our constant urge to escape from our limitations, our feeling that knowledge and indeed all activity is defeated and negated in so far as it comes up against a limit, our fantasies of omniscience, omnipotence and self-sufficiency. True, these are fantasies. We cannot imaginatively realise what it would truly be like to be such a being. And yet there is something in our nature, in our conscious and intelligent nature, which rebels at the thought of a limit. In a word, we have here the paradoxical case of a concept which is founded partly on our experience and partly on our aspiration to transcend our experience – which aspiration is also an experience. The concept points beyond experience in a certain direction, along a scale whose lowest degrees can actually be seen in the empirical world.

WHEREOF WE CANNOT SPEAK?

Religion has constantly maintained that behind everything, when we come to the ultimate source of everything, we find a mystery. Philosophical theology has often appeared to say the same, and has spelled out reasons for it. It will be worth while to spend a little time scrutinising these reasons.

It is said, for example, that the very form in which we express our thoughts makes them incapable of declaring the truth about God. We cannot make a statement except in subject–predicate form, and in God there is no distinction between subject and attributes. We cannot think or speak except discursively, and discursive language cannot describe the being of God. These arguments are less than convincing, for after all the verbal form in which we make assertions does not determine the nature of what we assert. We can quite well say in subject–predicate form that God is not distinguishable into subject and attributes. We can quite well say discursively that God's being is not successive. The objector himself must do so in order to state his objection.

The same applies when we are told that God cannot be placed in a class or brought under a principle. God is metaphysically unique, but that need not prevent us from making him, for logical purposes, the member of a class which has only one member. God is not an instance of any general principle, but we can quite well infer from premises that he is not so.

Again, we may be told that though we can catalogue a few of God's attributes (if the expression may be excused), we cannot know his essence, i.e. we cannot see the necessary coherence of his attributes, why they must be just as they are and not otherwise. But we are in no better case with created things, and we do not make a song about their incomprehensibility; we accept what we can achieve and call that knowledge.

It cuts nearer the bone when we are told that we have no predicates which can rightly be applied to God; for (it is said) all our concepts are derived by abstraction from experience, and all empirical objects are finite. All our concepts, therefore, are of finite things, and inapplicable to God.

Let us assume for the moment that this is true. What follows?

One possible conclusion is the doctrine of the 'negative way'. Since all concepts which we can form are false in application to God, our only way to speak truly about him is to say so, to say that he is not this, not that, and so on indefinitely.

But it is felt that this doctrine is too rigorous. There are degrees of falsity, and it is certainly more false to say that God is foolish than to say that he is wise. Indeed, it is more false to say that God is not wise than to say that he is; and therefore it seems as if we ought to make the latter assertion, despite the element of falsity in it, in order to exclude the greater falsity of its contradictory. And so a purely negative way is inacceptable.

But how can we with a good intellectual conscience make affirmative statements about God which we know are in the last resort false?

Here is the place of the doctrine of analogical predication, which is generally thought of in connection with the name of St Thomas Aquinas; though he is only one, the most famous one, among many scholastic philosophers who have canvassed the question. I shall try here briefly to extract the essential points.

'Analogy' is a word which has a variety of meanings, but the root meaning in Greek is 'proportion'. To say that an attribute can be predicated of God analogically is to say that it can be predicated of him not directly and without qualification, but by virtue of, and in the manner permitted by, some relation in which God stands to created things which have it. God stands in a relation R to a created thing C; the created thing C has an attribute A; and by virtue of the relation between God and the thing C we can infer an attribute A^1 in God which is not identical with, but related analogically to, the attribute A in the created thing.

This formula is applied in two principal ways.

In the first place, if we know God exists at all, we know he is the cause of the existence of everything that is not himself, and the cause of its having the attributes which it has. It is often said that things derive from him whatever reality they have. Whatever attributes a created thing may have, these attributes have their ultimate origin in God.

But how? Can we predicate the attributes of created things directly of God? In most instances evidently not. God is not red, or square, or a ruminant. He has in himself whatever is necessary to create things with these attributes, but the attributes themselves, as attributes, he does not possess. And yet there are some attributes of created things which we do not hesitate to predicate of God as characterising him, e.g. life, intelligence, knowledge, wisdom, will, goodness, freedom, personality. Two questions arise: how do we know which attributes of created things can really be said to characterise God? and how *can* they characterise him, incurably tainted as they are with finitude?

They cannot, strictly speaking. But here comes in the second and more subtle interpretation of the principle of analogy.

It should be recognised that an attribute, while remaining essentially the same attribute, can appear in different forms according to the different kinds of things which it characterises. For example, a man and a cabbage are both living things, but the livingness of a cabbage is very different from the livingness of a man, and the difference between the two kinds of livingness is determined by, and in a sense proportional to, the difference between the sort of being that a man is and the sort of being that a cabbage is. Life is an analogical attribute as between man and cabbage. It is the same and yet not the same. Now, the same principle applies wherever an attribute characterises both God and a created thing.

Thus some men are wise, and God is wise. Wisdom is analogical as between God and man – the same and yet not the same. That attribute in God which we call his wisdom is very different from wisdom as we find it in men; and the part which it plays in his life, its relation to God's other attributes and to the whole being of God, are all different from their analogues in men. And the difference is determined by, or proportioned to, the difference between the kind of being that God is and the kind of being that a man is. It is proportioned to the difference between infinite and finite. And so the correct analysis of the proposition 'God is wise' would be 'there is an attribute W which is, in the being of God, analogous to what wisdom is in the being of a man'.

On this showing, since we know what wisdom is in man, we could know what it is in God if we knew how God's nature is related to ours. And verbally, of course, we do know this. We know that God is to us as infinite to finite. But here is the difficulty. For, according to the theory which we are considering, all our concepts are tainted with finitude, and therefore we can never know what any attribute is at infinity. We come to a dead stop.

So far, then, the theory of analogical predication has not shown us how any predicate which we can conceive can be true of God. Nor has it answered the other of our two questions: how we can tell which predicates can rightly be taken as characterising God and not merely his creatures.

The answer to both questions is the same. Perhaps there are after all some predicates which do not entail finitude. If so, these will be the ones which can properly be attributed to God, and this will be why they can be so attributed.

This answer was made to St Thomas in his own time. Both St Bonaventura and Duns Scotus recognised that concepts such as knowledge or will, wisdom or goodness, do not entail finitude, even though all instances of them which fall within our experience are finite. Indeed we feel that the finitude is a kind of negation of that to which it attaches. A limited goodness is not altogether goodness, a limited knowledge is to that extent a non-knowledge. The true meaning of these terms, we feel, would only be realised in infinity; and though the human mind cannot hope to understand realisingly what these things are at infinity, it can make some not insignificant steps in the right direction. Something similar might be said of concepts like life, activity, perhaps even being itself in one sense of that multivalent word.

If there is truth in what we have just said, then the doctrine of analogy does not lead to an impasse, but on the contrary it formulates in its own characteristically scholastic terms the process by which we really do succeed in reaching a positive conception of God. Only let it be remembered that this does not mean a clear-cut concept which we could fully explicate and in which the mind could rest as in an achieved truth. Rather it means something like the dialectical process we went through in the previous section of this chapter, feeling our way to some notion of the infinite by successive denials of the finite. This process needs to be continually renewed, because the element of finitude in our conceptions, however often expelled, will always return, like those transcendental illusions of which Kant speaks, which, however often exposed, keep on arising afresh, and need to be continually re-exposed by a continual renewal of the transcendental critique. Our conceiving of God is really a perpetually renewed attempt to conceive, leading to glimpses of a meaning which we can never retain for long and must continually strive to regain. And yet this is not nothing. It is indeed so much that, when once the mind is trained to it, it cannot tear itself away from the ever-repeated exercise. Paradoxical as it sounds, this restless movement of self-transcendence is its way of resting in God.

This Beyond, which we conceive by failing to conceive and of which we speak by failing to speak, is central in the teaching of historic Platonism, and of the Mahayana. And here, while purely philosophical arguments may be advanced as part of the exposition, there is clearly something more, a metaphysical drive, an ontological drawing to the Beyond. This term, 'beyond', is part of the vocabulary of both traditions. Plato's ultimate, the Good, is beyond knowledge though he/it is that to which all knowledge points; and he/it neither is nor is known, because he/it is the transcendent source of all that is and is known. The Neoplatonic One is 'beyond being'. The Ultimate in some Mahayana texts is called Suchness, a non-commital term and yet suggestive of absoluteness, and the way to it is by the systematic negation of the things of this world and even the alleged realities of elementary Buddhist teaching. We are to go beyond; the Heart Sutra sums up the 'perfection of wisdom' in a mantra which begins with the words 'gone, gone, gone beyond, gone utterly beyond'. These doctrines have a vertiginous attraction, very different from the conviction produced by a well-argued philosophical thesis. Yet it is not the attraction of sheer emptiness of nothingness, even though 'emptiness' is a favourite word in the Prajnaparamita. Plato's ultimate is called the Good. The Buddhist Suchness is the same which in other Buddhist traditions is called the Buddha-nature, and is mythologically figured in the Lotus Sutra as the Eternal Buddha. Both the Platonic and the Buddhist ultimate are objects of aspiration; one could say of them what St Bonaventura says of God, that 'his intelligibility is beyond all understanding, but he is utterly to be desired'.

STARING WITH A WILD SURMISE

And yet I do not think we have touched the bottom of the doctrine of the incomprehensibility of God. I believe that behind it there lies something further which is not a philosophical theorem at all, but an experience deriving from an attitude to things which is entirely different from that of philosophical enquiry.

Once or twice, in recent discussion among philosophers, reference has been made to the question why anything exists at all. The question is unanswerable, and from a logical point of view should be ruled out of order. But it is possible to know that and yet to find it a haunting question, and one which brings with it an atmosphere of awe.[1]

In my own way I know something like this awe. I know well enough that the question why anything exists at all is a nonsense question. The 'why' in it is not a genuine why, because there is no conceivable statement or set of statements beginning with 'because' which could be an answer to it. But this knowledge does not necessarily prevent the question from teasing the mind. 'God' is not an answer to it; he, if he be granted to exist, only explains why there is the universe, but then the question why there is anything at all re-emerges as the question why there is God. True, we construct God as an ultimate in the series of contingencies and conditionalities, and here therefore one might expect the questioning to stop. The reason why we sought an explanation for the universe was that it is a system of contingencies, which require a Non-contingent to make them actual; and so by definition, it would seem, the same question cannot arise about the Non-contingent itself. Perhaps not; but although we talk of God as the Non-contingent, it seems that this can only be true in a relative and limited sense. God is not subject to any of those conditions which govern the contingent things in his world, he is not subject to any conditions at all; but still in the last resort the fact that there is God, and not sheer nothing, is itself the ultimate contingency. God is not, as theism has so often improperly asserted, a (or the) Necessary Being. He is the Original Un-necessary, the Ultimate Sheer Fact. And in fact of this we are petrified with an astonishment tinged with awe.

Linked with the mystery of the thereness of things is the mystery of their suchness. The cover of this book before me is green. Why is it green? Someone made it so. Yes, but why was he able to make it so? Why is there such a colour as green at all? God conceived and created it. Well, in that case the reason is hidden somewhere in the depths of the divine being. God is such that he has created a world in which there are green things. But *why* is God such that he has created a world in which there are green things? What kind of a

[1] See J. J. C. Smart, in *New Essays in Philosophical Theology* (1955) pp. 18 f., 46.

'because' could possibly be offered in answer to this?

When the mind reaches this point it is not confronting an unknowable object, which is still an object of enquiry although unknowable, but has reached the point where its drive to obtain knowledge through enquiry, through questioning and answering, meets its limit in a meaningless question. At this point there is no possibility open but that of contemplation and wonder: not that rational wonder which leads to questions and experiments and is the driving force of science, but that still wonder which is the mind's attitude in face of sheer Being, a compound of acknowledgement, admiration and awe. And it is a contemplation which is bound to remain, even as a contemplation, partial and frustrated. What we should like is to see (not merely conceive) the sheer being of things with such clarity, fullness and intimacy that we should find here *il ben dell' intelletto*, that in which the mind could repose without any urge to ask or seek further. We should like to see ourselves at that point where reasons cease because they vanish in the Fact. But that would be the beatific vision, which comes to no one in this life. Deprived of that, we hang in an indecisive position, finding no repose in a contemplation which is so meagre in content, and trying instinctively to find satisfaction by continuing to enquire, yet unable to frame any question but this senseless one, why existence is as it is, and why anything exists at all. And being out of our depth, we feel awe.

This too must be counted as part of what is meant by the incomprehensibility of God.

8 Not Proven

After exploring some of the ramifications of the classical arguments, let us return and consider the substance of the arguments themselves. Do they prove their point? And first of all: both the contingency argument and argument from design are metaphysical constructions based on a doctrine of the nature of being. Both argue that, since the nature of being is what it is, certain things which undoubtedly exist could not exist if it were not that God exists also. Are we compelled to embrace this conclusion?

METAPHYSICAL REALISM

Yes, if ontological dependence is a real relation and not just a phrase which we use. Yes, if we really know what can or cannot, could or could not be, as distinct from what is. The classical arguments rest on the assumption that we can do this. They rest on what I shall call a metaphysical realism, i.e. a belief that the human mind can penetrate by sheer reasoning to that than which nothing is more real. Not that we can reach a full comprehension of this reality, but that we can discern its nature sufficiently to enable us to describe it with confidence.

We hear of realism sometimes in modern philosophy; but here it mostly means some kind of a reply to Berkeley, an assertion that the *esse* of perceived objects neither is nor is derived from their *percipi*. If the great metaphysical thinkers of past times did not assert this anti-Berkeleian thesis or argue in its support, it is because they never thought of doubting it. What I am here calling their realism is something different from this. Of course things exist and are what they are independently of being perceived or known by us or by any finite intelligence; but the point is that we can also know what they are. However much may depend upon the mind's activity in perceiving and imagining, in verbalising, generalising, judging, theorising and the like, still the result to which all this leads is that our intellect looks through the sensory appearance and takes hold of the real natures of things. And it does not matter if the appearance of things depends to some extent upon the body or mind of the perceiver, or if the terms in which he apprehends their natures are conditioned by his linguistic and logical equipment. It does not matter if, being finite, he does not know all that there is to be known about things. It is natural enough that the knower should know things according to his own powers and limitations, but a partial knowledge is still knowledge, and genuine knowledge is possible to us even in the realm of metaphysical ultimates. Such is the common assumption of the writers of the great tradition. It is realism in something more like the mediaeval than the modern sense of the word – a trust in the explorations and constructions of the human intellect.

In its light the questions which philosophy addresses to theism are confidently answered. Knowing the natures of things, not completely but still truly, we are able to find the pattern of relationships, the underlying structure on which these natures are based. The pattern of contingencies in the empirical world is such that by following it out we can detect the ultimate dependence of the world on God. And however remote from experience may be the terms in which God has to be conceived, it does not follow that they are beyond intelligibility; for, as it is the structure of experience as a whole which demands God's existence, so too the concept of God is found by operating with elements which have all been found first in experience.

Modern philosophy shows itself less and less disposed to take so much for granted. This is due to a tendency towards greater rigour, a greater insistence on clarity in statement and cogency in argument in anything that is to count as knowledge. Such a tendency is not confined to modern philosophy, however widely we may define that term. It appeared also in the final phase of mediaeval scholastic philosophy, and there also it led to hesitations about the natural theology which the earlier mediaevals had built up. In our time it challenges not only the force of the arguments used in this realm, but also the meaning of some of the terms used in them.

There is no need to go to the extreme of saying that what we know owes its existence to our knowing of it. Any theory which involves that is an eccentricity and misses the real point. What we know is real being; but while we can claim with fair confidence to have a growing knowledge of particular things and kinds of things which present themselves in our experience, we can form no certain and definitive doctrine of the most general structure of being, the fundamental properties and relationships which underlie the empirical manifold. Philosophers have spoken of these matters in the past with a confidence which we now see was not justified.

For common-sense purposes things and their relations are much as they appear, and we are able to understand them as an orderly world in which we are at home. But as our knowledge grows it becomes increasingly clear that the sensible qualities of things are relative to our human sense-equipment and the conditions under which it operates. When physical science draws its picture of the real structure of matter, it is drawn in purely quantitative terms; we can form no conception of the qualitative nature of what we are dealing with, only of the movements and interactions of its parts. Even such formal structures as space and time reveal themselves to the physicist as different from what we perceive, and beyond what we can imagine. We know them only in a purely symbolic way, in terms of mathematical formulae. Yet even so we can detect amid these abstractions the equivalents of what we know phenomenally as events and processes, process-patterns and relations of dependence.

But what, after all, do we mean by this word 'dependence'?

It seems that we mean something to do with ontological necessity, in other words that some things must be, and some things cannot be, because of the being of other things. We talk like this in ordinary discourse as if we knew what it meant, and metaphysicians in the classical tradition were so sure they knew what it meant that they argued on the strength of it to the enormous conclusion which theism is. But analysis shows clearly enough that we have no idea what it means. We can see tolerably well how things are, so far as our experience ranges, but we cannot see that they must be as they are. For example, when we speak of a contingent being, as distinct from a contingent proposition, we mean a being which 'cannot' exist unless something causes it to exist. The existence of a contingent being is dependent on the action of its cause. But what is this action of its cause? What is it for a cause to act? To this question no answer can be given. We know in ourselves, from within, what it feels like to come under an influence or a constraint, and we know what it feels like to be an agent in action. But that is not the same thing as apprehending a necessary relation between cause and effect. All we know about that is that by observation and experiment we find recurrent patterns of process in things. By scientific enquiry we learn what are the prevailing patterns in the realm of each particular science. Within a particular pattern we recognise that A 'depends upon' B in the sense that that is the way the pattern works – the occurrence of A is always linked in a certain way with the occurrence of B. But in all this we are merely registering what we find to be the case; we are not understanding that it must be, nor are we entitled to say that what we find could not be if it were not for something else which our investigations never disclose. The only evidence for what can be is the empirical fact of what is, and that does not take us beyond the sphere of the experimentally verifiable into the realm of what cannot be experimentally checked or even precisely defined.

If this analysis is correct, the arguments from contingency and from design do not prove the existence of God.

THE METAPHYSIC OF INTELLIGIBILITY

But there is also the argument which proceeds not by investigating what we find to be the case, but by explicating what must be the case if reality is to be intelligible to us. Here is the same metaphysical realism as before, but in a more confident and challenging form. However sceptically we may talk, our practice shows us all to be convinced that to explain phenomena, to render them intelligible, is the way to find the truth about them. On the phenomenal level, in dealing with the empirical world, we work on this principle, and must, for there is no alternative. The metaphysician summons us to be boldly consistent and to push our principle beyond the empirical world into the sphere of ultimates. If in that sphere, beyond all possibility of observation, no detailed information can be had, a knowledge of things in principle is possible none the less. For the ultimate in reality must be also the ultimate in intelligibility. Enough, then, to show that the ultimate in intelligibility is personality, self-contained and yet self-expressive; that established, it is also established that an absolute personality is the ultimate reality of things.

The argument, however, takes much for granted. Is an explanation in terms of personality really more satisfactory to the intellect than an explanation in the natural-scientific mode? At least all explanations in natural science can be checked by objective evidence, whereas with these all-comprehending speculative theories there is no such check. And if in science no explanation is ever complete or final, does that really mean that we are justified in looking to pure speculation in search of an account of things which is such that we cannot even wish to go beyond it? And is theism really such an account of things? In view of the now so well known difficulties attending upon theist doctrines, can theism possibly be regarded as 'satisfying the demands' of the intellect? Only, perhaps, if the final demand of the intellect is for its own transcendence; a doctrine which indeed Plato and Plotinus and Bradley were not afraid to teach.

One must admire the boldness with which this philosophy sets out to scale the heights. Yet on sober reflection one must also admit that the principle on which it rests, that the real is that which satisfies the demands of the intellect, is a piece of unsupported dogmatism outstripping even the metaphysical realism which we found underlying the earlier arguments. For that only claimed that we can trace the patterns of reality in our experience and can reach truth by extrapolating them beyond experience; but this newer philosophy, not content to say that our mind can detect reality, defines reality as that which our mind requires. To those who asserted this – so recently in years, yet it seems such an age ago – it seemed the voice of reason itself. And perhaps even today some survivor somewhere may ask us how we know that it is not true. We do not know. Neither do we know that it is true; and that is the point.

One can see whence it arises, and how in a sense we all live in the faith that it is true. For constructing coherent patterns is the way our minds work, they cannot work any other way, and the disposition to believe a coherent story to be true is built into our constitution. It plays an indispensable part in scientific reasoning; for it is not enough, for scientific purposes, to have observed a great variety of phenomena and catalogued them accurately; one must also make a coherent story of them, or the work of science is not done. But on the other hand, this capacity which we have for constructing coherent patterns is not necessarily correlated with reality. If it plays a necessary part in science, it is also at the root of art and every kind of fantasy. Our efficiency in reality-seeking has grown in proportion as we have learned to employ our system-constructing power only in conjunction with observation and experiment, and to believe no story, however good, which has not empirical evidence in its favour. That is how scientific method has come into our thinking. But in theology we are outside the range of scientific enquiry. Theology begins only when science has shot its bolt, and proceeds by the old method of looking for a coherent account to give of things, without either the rigour of reasoning or the experimental checks which science has. True, it can do no other if it is to exist at all, but just here is the question: has theology a right to exist at all?

BEYOND METAPHYSICAL ARGUMENT

And yet the idealists were right in a way. We may say that all we can ever know of things is a loose-ended system in which our understanding is always relative and partial, but we cannot help sometimes wondering whether that is really all. We cannot help asking whether the universe may not be a closed system of interactions and interdependences, all deriving from one absolute source, and whether such a system may not have some sort of a meaning for us who live in it. And there is the God-vision which shows us, admittedly in figurative terms, how that might be. One source, one design, one meaning for life – that is what it offers us. But if we cannot help asking the question, neither can we help bringing the answer under scrutiny. As F. H. Bradley once wrote in epigrammatic vein, 'Metaphysics is the finding of bad reasons for what we believe upon instinct, but to find these reasons is no less an instinct'. In other words, if there is an instinct to believe, there is no less an instinct to seek reasons in support of the belief. And what then is to happen if the reasons, being themselves scrutinised in turn, are found to be 'bad reasons', devoid of logical cogency and in the last resort doubtfully meaningful? Are we to give up our instinctive belief because we have failed to rationalise it? Or shall we continue to believe 'upon instinct', while of course being careful not to mistake our instinctive belief for knowledge?

Many theists in fact believe on grounds which have nothing to do with the metaphysical arguments, which they have not seriously studied, and whose collapse causes them no dismay. They believe because of the life-relevance of theism which we encountered in Chapter 7. This flows both from the personal analogy under which God is conceived, and from the mystery of his incomprehensibility. From the personal aspect flow value-standards, directives, a whole drama of relationships and interactions between God and ourselves; and in the mystery we find escape from finitude, even from our own finitude, and satisfaction of our impulse towards self-transcendence. The relevance of all this for human life provides a reason for indulging our instinct to believe the God-vision.

What kind of a reason for believing this is, we shall examine later in Chapter 13. But the belief which it serves to justify has interesting experiential consequences. It has given rise to a many-featured tradition of self-training and discipline in the spiritual life, by which a whole new world of experience is opened up for our exploration. This is the world of religious experience, and many people argue from it, putting it forward as a kind of experimental verification of what God-belief asserts and promises. Here is something which found no place in the metaphysical reasonings of the traditional natural theologians. But it was always present in the mind of the ordinary believer, and played a prominent part in preaching and propaganda as distinct from systematic reasoning about God. In recent times, with the gradual discredit of the metaphysical arguments and the spread of an empiricist temper in the world, attempts have been made to argue formally from the facts of religious experience to God as their source.

Religious experience in one aspect or another will be the subject of my next three chapters.

Part III
RELIGIOUS
EXPERIENCE
AND FAITH

9 Modes of Experiential Contact with God

So far the customary arguments for the existence of God. But many God-believers would say that their belief does not rest on argument, but on an awareness of being somehow in touch with God through their experience. This raises the question of what is called religious experience and the part which it plays in generating and maintaining God-belief. What kind of experience is it? Is it a perception? Is God presented in it as an object, from the perception of which empirical concepts can be formed? Is that the real source and origin of God-belief? Or if not, what kind of experience is religious experience and what cognitive value can be claimed for it?

THE GAMUT OF RELIGIOUS EXPERIENCE

Religious experience is of very various kinds, but in none of them is God directly perceived as an object, though there is always what is taken to be an awareness of his presence and activity. The basic form of it is to be found in the God-vision described above in Chapter 5. There the God-seer perceives, or seems to himself to perceive, the activity of God at the heart of all that is and all that happens, and he will often say that he 'sees' God in these things. So he does, in one legitimate sense of the world 'see'; but God is not present to him as an object of direct perception. All that is present to him in that mode is physical things and events. Into these he reads, with intuitive immediacy and unhesitating confidence, the presence and activity of the All-Agent, very much as we read the presence and activity of human minds into the bodily forms and movements which are all that is actually presented to us for perception.

I have already shown how in the vision of the All-Agent lies the genesis of 'God', how the vision becomes elaborated into mythologies and rationalised into theologies, until finally the standard figure of 'God' emerges. Here at the beginning, religious experience in the form of the imaginative God-vision is the foundation on which the whole structure of God-doctrine is ultimately built. But the theological doctrine, once established and elaborated, reacts upon our experience, and the more developed forms of religious experience are the result of our reactions to the doctrine, our attempts to work it out in life. We find ourselves drawn into a kind of personal intercourse with God, which becomes more and more intimate as we progress in the spiritual life. It opens up perspectives of a kind of life far transcending the every-day horizon of the ordinary man, even the ordinary intelligent and moral man. All this constitutes the realm of what is called religious experience. Not every God-believer has all forms of it. Many speak as if they have, or think they have, none at all; their religion is their ethic, backed up by a belief in its supernatural warrant. But others, again, seem deeply initiated in it, and what they say and do affects the intellectual and spiritual atmosphere for others besides themselves.

The most primitive reaction to God is the emotional response of awe. It is an emotion to which some people are more susceptible than others. Like other emotions, it is subject to a degree of control; one can resist feeling it, or one can throw oneself open to it. But essentially it is a passive experience, a response to something perceived or imagined. 'Experience', however, does not mean only seeing and feeling; it also means learning about things by seeking and finding and interacting with them, by enquiry and experiment. This is the true meaning of *experior*, and the man who has made his enquiries and learned his lessons is the *expertus*, the experienced man. Religious experience has this exploratory and experimental dimension too; there is a religious way of living and an expertise in it. There is a kind of 'knowledge' of God which is gained through a sustained active contact with him in the events and actions of one's life ('walking with God' in the Old Testament phrase); and there is a peculiar 'contemplative' kind of awareness of God, sometimes associated with a kind of perceptual awareness, not of God in himself, but of his action in the soul.

It is a wide field, which has been deeply studied and fully documented. Here I can give only a brief (though, I hope, a balanced) survey. So much I must do, or there will be a gap in the picture I am drawing of how 'God' functions in human thought and life.

LEARNING ABOUT GOD FROM THE EXPERIENCE OF LIFE

To learn experimentally one requires a working hypothesis, which is to be applied and tested and modified in the light of results. True, we are able from our earliest years to learn by experience of things and people without consciously forming hypotheses or knowing anything of the logic of experimental enquiry. But we apply its principles without knowing that we are doing so. Similarly it is probable that most religious people have no very clear methodological awareness; nevertheless they have their working principles, and we can show what these are.

Let us begin with what is believed about the nature of God and the nature of man. Since we as intelligent personalities are in some degree akin to God, we may venture to suppose that there can be some kind of personal or quasi-personal relationship between him and us. This would naturally depend on our cultivating that in us which is most akin to God and responsive to any communication that may come from him. The characteristically religious life-pattern is one of endeavouring to do this; though the details of the way, and the nature of the goal, are differently presented in different doctrines.

It is possible to hold that man's relation to God is essentially communal, maintained by public rituals performed according to a regular pattern and by the observance of certain standards of behaviour in the community. Such is the meaning of all official state cults. There may be adherents of many religious traditions who are content with their share in the communal approach to God and who ask nothing more. What interests us, however, is the individual's relation with God in his own life.

Such a relation is implicit in the vision of God as All-Agent. For, if all that is and happens is his doing, then in seeing anything I am seeing not merely that thing, taken *cum praecisione*, but something in which God is manifesting, something which he is showing to me. In my recognition of this, my appreciation of the work and my acknowledgment of its Author, there is already a relationship, a kind of shared experience between him and me. One can get into the habit of sharing experiences with him in this way.

But the relation becomes richer and more significant when I am confronted with a situation requiring that I should act, or at least that I should deliberately take up an attitude. If God is All-Agent, all the facts which together constitute my situation are his work. He made them, he brought about the situation, and he brought me into the situation. If it demands of me action or decision, it is he who through the situation demands these things of me. But further, I myself am his work, with my needs and desires and ideals and principles. These are not what they would be if I were morally and spiritually more mature, but, such as they are, they are the guide-lines which he gives me in this situation here and now. If I interpret the guide-lines wisely and follow them honestly, my judgment will be clearer and firmer next time. If I fail to achieve my purpose, if disconcerting results follow, then either my choice of means was unwise, or I may have got the wrong directives; or I may have thought too readily that if I do the right thing I am entitled to expect success. That may not be God's way of governing events or of disciplining me. And so through reflections like these I may grow in wisdom and insight. The moral life is at the same time an education; it is a life in which we gain fuller understanding as we act on the understanding which we have. And all this in a relationship with God, a relationship which matures as we mature.

SERVANTS AND FRIENDS OF GOD

It need hardly be said that God-believers are not the only people who can learn from experience in this way. Anyone who genuinely cares for values, and who at the same time is willing to revise his formulae from time to time in the light of experience, can do so. But where the conscious relationship with God is present there arises a recognisable type of religious outlook and constellation of religious ideas. The believer is likely to think of right actions as demands made upon him or commands issued to him by God, and of the principles of right conduct as a divine law. He will think of God as king, lord or master, and of himself as the servant of God, whose central motive is or should be obedience. No one can go far in reading religious literature without becoming familiar with this set of ideas. And we must not suppose that the idea of being under a divine law or subject to divine commandments is necessarily felt as a constraint or arouses resentment in the believer. The 119th Psalm is striking evidence to the contrary, and is far from standing alone. The relationship gives to the servant of God a status in the scheme of things and a sense of order and direction in life. If the habit of obedience is combined with an unqualified acceptance of all fortune which God sends, simply because it is what God sends, it constitutes that total self-surrender which Muhammad calls Islam and which he makes the foundation of all true religion. The Jew and the Christian and the Hindu *bhakta* will agree that he is right in this.

No one ever grows out of being God's obedient servant; but one may grow to be much else as well. There are degrees of intimacy in our relations with God, and the New Testament teaches us that beyond the status of servant there is that of a friend. One begins to move towards it when, besides thinking of God's law and obeying it, one begins to think of God himself, not only with awe but with wonder, admiration, gratitude, joy and a kind of love. True, as one comes to compare oneself more closely with him, one may begin to feel one's own insignificance, and beyond that, one's sinfulness and unworthiness, and that may erect a barrier for a time in the way of contact with him. But the religions have ready antidotes for this condition. Christianity in particular, which can sometimes arouse in its adherents a quite overwhelming sense of guilt, has also a reconciliation technique embodied in a salvation-story of incomparable power. So one learns to forget oneself a little and to think of God instead, and to live with him freely and without hesitation or constraint. One sees God more clearly in things, and becomes gradually somewhat detached from created things and finite goods, not as despising them, but as knowing that which is better than they. Something like this is what St Francis de Sales calls 'the devout life' in his book of that title. Ruysbroeck, who also analyses it at length, adopts the New Testament phrase and calls it the life of God's friends.

Beyond the servant and the friend – the lover. In all the religions there are those who boldly call themselves God's lovers. This is the highest grade of intimacy; degrees within it there may be and are, but no degree beyond it. But this brings us to the subject of mysticism.

MYSTICISM AND MYSTICAL EXPERIENCE

Here I must define my terms, since the word 'mysticism' is used in such a variety of sense. I use it here to signify the drive of the human soul towards an experiential intimacy, often described as union, with what is ultimate in things – 'God' or whatever else it may be called. The mystic is one who sees the deep-seated unity which things have by virtue of their common derivation from and utter dependence upon the Ultimate, and who wishes to be drawn experientially nearer to the Centre of that unity than he is now.

This definition leaves room for variety, and variety there is. Different doctrines are put forward among mystics and students of mysticism. The very goal of the quest, the 'union' with the Ultimate, is conceived in different ways. The discipline of the way, the states and experiences which occur along it, are again differently described. Some schools of thought define or describe mysticism in terms which other schools would repudiate. In particular, mysticism is often described in terms which make it incompatible with theism.

For example, the prevailing strand of thought in the Vedanta teaches that all souls are essentially identical with the Ultimate, though most of us do not know this, and that the goal of the spiritual quest is not properly a union, but the acquisition of an experimental awareness of a unity which already exists. Others, while not saying that the human self is originally identical with God, say that in the course of the mystical life it is so drawn into God as to be 'lost' or 'absorbed' in his being; the analogy of a drop of water falling into the ocean is sometimes used. Such doctrines, if literally meant, would be incompatible with standard theism. No one who adhered to the standard western pattern of doctrine could consistently say that the finite self essentially 'is' God or that it is 'absorbed' into him. A created thing it is and will always remain, though it may become more and more intimately related to God by way of loving adherence; and that is the 'union' of which theist mysticism or mystical theism speaks.

My difficulty with the identity and absorption doctrines is in understanding what they mean. On the face of it the finite self is very different from what we mean by 'God'; and when I am told that they are identical, I need more information than I am given as to how this is to be interpreted. As for absorption, it is a physical metaphor, and the soul is not a physical thing. Of course one could also think of a psychological analogy, the soul becoming so 'absorbed' in the contemplation of God that the consciousness of distinctness is overwhelmed and individual personality is thus lost. But the popularity of the physical analogy is puzzling. And when in Hindu devotional literature I find identity language, absorption language and loving-union language used side by side in the works of one author, or when I find absorption language in Charles Wesley, who unquestionably would have repudiated any attempt to make it mean what it says, I am entitled to wonder whether all is as it sounds. Anyone who has experience of the intenser forms of love between human beings will know how easily absorption language and even identity language can spring to the lips at certain moments; but he will also know how far this is from what the lovers really experience and really desire. For love is a reciprocity of life which simply cannot occur where there are not two distinct parties.

In any case this is not a book on mysticism, but on theism, and mysticism comes in only as it refers to 'God' and strives towards union with him. Therefore it is only that mysticism whose goal is a union of love which is of interest to us. The richest and best documented tradition of this kind of mysticism is the Christian tradition.

In this tradition the aspirant, having already learned to follow the way of obedience and the way of the devout life, seeks the closest possible union with God by way of love. As he progresses, as his mind becomes more and more concentrated upon God and relatively detached from finite things, it is natural that he should arrive at forms of thought and experience which are unknown to the ordinary man or even to the ordinary devout man. Consciousness assumes different modes when it is firmly directed upon a different kind of object from any in the empirical world. The apprehension of God and the approach to him in meditation and prayer become increasingly immediate and intuitive. With the growing awareness that he transcends all images and all concepts, the mind dwells less upon words and ideas and finds ways of reaching after the inapprehensible. Of these, again I shall say only what bears upon my present argument.

Mystics are popularly credited with seeing, or at any rate claiming to see, things which the ordinary man does not discern. And so they do.

(a) Their strong conviction of the inner unity of things is essentially no more than an intense form of that God-vision which I described in a previous chapter; but the discipline to which the mystic subjects himself can only tend to sharpen that vision and make it count for more in the totality of his experience.

(b) Meditation and self-analysis lead naturally to an understanding of the soul's life at a deeper level than most people achieve. The mystic finds himself talking the same sort of language as the depth psychologists and the existentialist philosophers. He finds something else as well, viz. that unobjectifiable deep centre of the self which in European spiritual writings has often been called the ground of the soul.

(c) Habitual meditation upon and contemplation of God can only bring a fuller awareness of the inherent obscurity of the concept. And what the philosopher and the theologian, analysing their way through, exhibit as logical Paradoxes or apparent contradictions embodying an intellectual challenge, the mystic, aiming always at an intuitive grasp of the whole, sees and accepts as mysteries within that whole. And because, unlike analytical philosophers and theologians, he is essentially a realist, he does not think much about the obscurity of the concept but rather about the inherent mysteriousness of the object. Darkness is a constant feature of his way; and while in the earlier stages he may speak of a darkness, or cloud, between himself and God, he passes on to the point where he sees that God himself is the darkness. This vision of invisibility is the point where he most clearly transcends common experience and thought.

In the language which the mystics themselves use to describe their awareness of God, while much is said in terms of vision (contemplation, illumination and so forth), use is also made of the vocabulary of touch. Not that I can reach out at will and touch God, but that God touches me and I can feel him do it. This kind of experience is found most strikingly in the mystics, but it is not confined to them. It is widespread among those who keep an attitude of 'openness' towards God.

The essence of the matter is a conscious passivity of the soul towards God, a consciousness of an impact made by God's action upon it. In Whitehead's language, it is an instance not of presentational immediacy, but of causal efficacy, felt from the passive side of the relationship.

There is a mode of experience in which the mind or soul is conscious of being subject to an influence which does not proceed from within the ego. This shows itself in the irruption of thoughts and impulses which have no antecedent in the previous conscious life of the subject. Sometimes they are of an undesirable kind; in such a case our ancestors would have ascribed them to evil spirits, while the fashionable view today ascribes them to the subject's own unconscious. But sometimes they are of a kind for which God is felt to be a more plausible explanation than either of these.

The belief that these experiences do not proceed from within the ego, but from another source, is not merely an inference from our inability to trace their antecedents. They come with a force which requires effort to meet it. Sometimes they can be dismissed with an effort. Sometimes they refuse to be dismissed. Sometimes, though rarely, they overwhelm all rival forces and bring about a change of mind in the subject, which may be radical and may prove lasting. That is one of the types of experience which we call a conversion. Or again, there may be a momentary suspension of the empirical consciousness, which is called ecstasy or rapture. In any case it is not merely a matter of thoughts which we find ourselves having, but of a dynamic interaction with someone or something.

In the religious sector it is first of all a matter of insights which come intuitively and impress themselves upon the mind with a feeling of luminosity and a sense of givenness. It is as if someone were lighting lamps in the soul. And then the soul begins to find that its manner of praying is subject to a control which is also an empowerment, so that, in praying or in contemplating God, the soul is not merely putting forth its own energies, but is at the same time being energised by a power which is not its own. And there are deeper and more obscure experiences, of which I shall only say that they are experiences of a union between God and the soul, so intimate that it fully explains (though it does not objectively justify) the occasional use of absorption language in describing it. In a word there are infinite modes and infinite degrees in the soul's passivity to God, and also in the soul's awareness of it, which is not the same thing. But always it is not a perception of God as an object, but the felt touch of God as an agent; not in the presentational mode, but in that of causal efficacy.

THE EVIDENTIAL VALUE OF RELIGIOUS EXPERIENCE

These various forms of God-experience commonly appear convincing to those who have them. They do not doubt the reality of what they see and feel, or the truth of their interpretation of it. But from a logical point of view what evidential value have these experiences?

A point in their favour is that they are in a sense communicable. It is clear that numbers of people speak and write about these things, that they understand one another, and that discussion can and does take place. On the other hand the conceptual system generally adopted by experients, and the relation between it and the common experience of mankind, will be found unsatisfactory.

Take first the experiences of the servants and friends and lovers of God, who perceive his presence and his guidance in and beyond the things and events of the world. It is only some people who are thus God-seers, and only they can understand what other God-seers say. Those who have seen the ground of the self know what it is to see the ground of the self. Those who have seen the divine darkness know what it is to see the divine darkness. Those who can see God in things know what it is to see God in things. They are sometimes heard to speak of others as blind, i.e. as lacking an essential capacity without which God-perception is not possible. Those who have the capacity thus appear to constitute a kind of elite, and what they know is not for all to know, but for those to whom it is given. The capacity needs developing, and within the God-seeing community those who are able to see at all can be effectively trained to see better; but an initial gift seems to be required, for whose absence training cannot compensate.

This might not matter so much if the conceptualisation of the experience led to a set of ideas which could stand up to logical tests. The concepts into which God-vision is translated would have to be clear, consistent, and logically related in some way to those of our accepted body of knowledge. But we know that this is not the case. We have been examining the concepts and have found them bewildering. Consideration of the experience underlying them certainly gives us the reason why some minds insist on inhabiting this perplexing country, but is no help towards showing that one meets with realities there.

A similar result emerges when we turn to the experiences of passivity, of feeling the touch of God. These experiences are too well attested for their occurrence to be doubted. They can be described and discussed, but only among those who have experienced something of the kind (not necessarily, however, in a high degree). Those who have felt the touch of God know what it is to feel the touch of God.

But, as we found before, the experience cannot be satisfactorily conceptualised; all the more as it has essentially no presentational element in it. All that it yields is a presence and a causal agency. True, we can argue from the effects which it produces that it has something to do with 'God'; but it remains, at least to the outside observer, a probable hypothesis that what is at work here is a deep unconscious drive in the soul, of which 'God' is a mythological projection. Those who have actually felt the touch are less likely to settle for this; they will be more apt to assert an Agent ontologically distinct from themselves. But even so, the form in which they think and speak of this Agent will be shaped by the God-image and God-concept which they have derived from other sources. It will not result directly from the experience itself.

In our perception of the sensible world, the particular sensory impression is of little use by itself. It needs to be synthesised with others, in such a way that the whole complex can be interpreted and given its place in our world-picture. We thus become aware of a whole system of objects, some which we recognise to be acting upon us in various ways. The recognition that this particular object is now acting upon me in this particular way can only take place in the context provided by a multiplicity of objects and a system of interpretative concepts. Now, where is the context and where is the framework of interpretative concepts into which the 'perception' of God's action upon my mind or soul can be fitted? The context can be no other than the whole course of my mental, moral and spiritual life, and the interpretative concepts can come from nowhere but from a pre-existing theology. In short, I must have already in my mind a concept of God such that it allows the possibility of such divine action upon the human soul, and I can then recognise a case of this action if it happens to me. It is true that I may not in the past have actually believed in the existence of such a God; and it may happen that an experience of the kind here under discussion activates the concept and leads me to say 'It was true, then, after all'. Here, then, in this way the experience acts as evidence, convincing me of the truth of what I had previously been told. But without the interpretative concept and the total experience of life with which that concept is integrated, the experience would be dumb, even to me the experient. All the more dumb must it be to the non-experient who only hears my mysterious description of it.

10 Being and Beyond Being

Theists assert that God is, or exists. But they do more than that. They define him in terms of being. He is *ens realissimum*. He is that being (there can only be one) whose essence and existence are the same. He is *ipsum esse*, not as an abstraction but as the most concrete of actualities, *ipsum esse subsistens*.

The fact that most of us nowadays do not do our thinking in terms of this philosophy does not dispense us from the trouble of understanding it. The writers who used these terms were not merely propounding a metaphysical theorem; they were saying something exciting and fascinating about God. How could this be? What is there that is exciting about calling God *ipsum esse*? That is what we must now explore. That is the subject of this chapter; not whether God exists, but what it is for God to exist, and especially what it is for God to be *ipsum esse*.

EXISTENCE AND THE NOT-SELF

But first of all we must clear out of the way the more ordinary use of the words 'be' or 'exist' viz. the use in which 'S exists' = 'there is such a thing as S' and is the contradictory opposite of 'S does not exist' or 'there is no such thing as S'. In predicating existence of S in this way we are not saying anything about S, but something about the sum of things, viz. that the sum of things includes S among its constituents, and something about our own situation, viz. that we are under a constraint to take account of S in our attempts at reality-thinking.

'Being' in this sense is univocal, as Duns Scotus pointed out in opposition to Aquinas. The Angelic Doctor had held that 'being' is necessarily an analogical term, because among the things which are there is a multiplicity of natures or being-styles which are ontologically analogous to one another. Analogical therefore must the term 'being' be. That would be true if the term 'being' referred to the natures or being-styles of things; but 'being' used in the sense we are now discussing says nothing about those. All it refers to is the thing they all have in common, which indeed is not anything at all about them but rather about us, viz. the necessity under which we are of reckoning with them.

The various things whose existence we affirm differ greatly both in their own natures and in the ways by which they come to our notice and are (so to speak) held in our minds. For example, sensible objects are directly present to us in their sensible qualities. For them, to exist entails a possibility of being perceived, and we know what it is like for them to be perceived, and can hold them in our imagination when they are absent. Not so the fundamental entities of physical theory. We can say a great deal about these, indeed the modern science of physics could not exist without them, but we cannot give a straight description of them as we can of sensible objects. When we think or speak of them, it is perforce on the analogy of sensibles; but we know no sensible qualities to ascribe to them, and even their spatio-temporal structure cannot be the same as the spatio-temporal structure of our perceived world. They are present to us as a set of formulae which can be correlated with sensible things, but we are unable to find a being-style which we could say was theirs. Despite these difficulties, it would be excessively odd to deny the reality or existence of these theoretical entities. Though we have no idea what it might be *in se* for such things to exist, we know what it is for us to have acknowledge them. Thus we affirm the existence both of sensible objects and of the theoretical entities, and in both cases we mean the same by 'existence', namely that in serious reality-thinking they have to be taken account of.

I have spoken of a constraint under which we find ourselves, a necessity of reckoning with certain things in any attempt at reality-thinking. This is not a logical necessity. An element of logical necessity may of course enter in where the object is known to us by virtue of scientific investigations and as part of a scientific theory. Then it is the logical force of the evidence which drives us and holds us to this particular conclusion. But behind this is the pre-logical constraint imposed by the empirical data, which are there whether we like it or not, and are what they are whether we like it or not, and which we have to acknowledge and respect.

Ordinarily we have no explicit consciousness of this constraint. We feel it at once when things obstruct our practical endeavours, but not when they merely channel our thoughts. Yet it is possible in moments of intense meditation to become intensely aware of it. I focus my attention on one object, say a stone, and contemplate it. It is here; it *is* here, no doubt about it, and would be here whether I thought so or not; it is as it is; I could think of endless other characteristics which it might have, but that would not affect it, it *is* as it is. Over against my freely moving thought it stands as something independent, obstacular, defiant (or so I feel). By obstinately being what it is it limits me, and the limitation can become, if I go on contemplating long enough, an intolerable strain, until I can no longer keep up the concentration and fly violently off to other thoughts.

Here is our primary apprehension of being; here is the basic force of the word 'is', in its predicative as well as in its existential sense. In either case it points to a confrontation between our thoughts and something which pays no regard to them, and to which they have to pay regard. Being is at first apprehended as over against us, as the found, the given, the other, the negation of our thoughts and desires, and of our very selves.[1] Conscious life is built on this experience. The whole life of a conscious being is a commerce with its other, with the not-self, and it is by successive responses to the not-self on successive levels of awareness that the self itself is built up.

When we speak of God as being, or existing, we of course mean what has here been explicated. He is obstinately there, he is obstinately what he is, and neither our thought nor our will can do anything about it. He is among those things of which we have to take account, and by our response to which our selfhood is shaped and characterised. But this is not all that we mean. Being, or existence, can be spoken of in a different sense which we must now explore.

BEING AS INWARDNESS

It is possible to speak of existence as something which we have or enjoy. We can speak of the joy of existence, and sometimes in the

---

[1] Our own being, of course, is as obstinate as that of external objects. It too is a reality which we have to reckon with. But we do not ordinarily contemplate it in the same way as we do external objects, and do not feel its obstinate independence in the same way. It is possible none the less to feel it and to feel constricted and fenced in by it; I shall speak of that experience later on.

language of devotion we express gratitude to God for giving us this joy – not merely for making our existence a joyful one, but for giving us existence, which is in itself a joy. When we talk like this, what we are thinking of is our own activity, the living activity of which we are conscious in ourselves, our being-style as conscious and self-conscious creatures.

Used in this way, 'to exist' is a verb of action. To exist is to energise, and we tend to think that whatever exists energises in a way somehow analogous to what we find in ourselves. We are tempted to think of physical objects as if they had an inner being of this kind, as if the not-self which stands over against us were something like an opposing will. This is surely a built-in illusion of our thought, analogous in its way to that built-in illusion of our perception which is called empathy. Yet it has often been worked up into a metaphysical theorem, as it was in their different ways by Spinoza and by Leibniz. The attempt, though constantly renewed, constantly fails to convince. The difficulties in detail of fitting an inner life into what we know to be the components of the physical world grow greater the more we learn about that world. But when we reach the higher animals and from them move up the scale to man, the case is different. Here we easily, and without doubt rightly, attribute to other persons an inner life and energy analogous to our own. The not-self here is another self, an other-self.

Our human life is a perpetual dialectic between the self and the surrounding other selves. Our relations with other people are far more important, for our development as persons, than our relations with the physical world. We are born into a world of people, we strive with always imperfect success to understand them and make ourselves understood by them, we become more and more involved with them in a web of relationships, competition and co-operation, friendship and enmity, love and hate. And always there is the teasing reflection that the not-self is also another self, that my own close kin stands over against me, challenges, combats or assists me, joins with me in love or puts up iron barriers against understanding and caring. In all around me I see myself, and in all too many I see myself estranged.

When we speak of God's being, we cannot help giving this meaning also to the phrase. God is not merely the absolutely inescapable Not-self, he is also the absolute Not-self which is the absolute Other Self. When we think of him as infinite or absolute being, we think of him as energising with absolute fullness, intensity and joy. This part of what we mean by his 'glory', sc. a splendour of experience which is dazzling and overwhelming to such of his creatures as may obtain even a glimpse of it, but which in himself is an absolute fullness of felicity.

When we think of God as All-Agent, it is in relation to the movements and changes which take place in the world. He is the Ultimate Mover of all that is in motion or in any process of change. We have seen how the mythopoeic imagination presents him as the Dancer, himself involved in the movements of his creatures. This of course can be accepted only as speaking of his effects *ad extra*, not of his inner being, which must be timeless and changeless and unlike any experience known to us finite beings and creatures of time. Even when in the ways of religious experience and the doctrines founded on it we appear to speak of God's thoughts and attitudes towards us, of the succession in him of good pleasure, wrath, and renewed good pleasure, of his plans and his actions in carrying them out, even then we are really talking about the way in which the course of events is guided with reference to us, and not about the inner being of the Agent.

We are not condemned to utter silence about that inner being, but everything we can rightly say must bring out the gulf between it and any experience of ours. Our being is mostly beyond our grasp; it is doled out to us in successive present moments, each hovering between a past which is no longer and a future which is not yet, and so we are never more than a fragment of our total selves. God's being must be a full possession of all that he has and is, with fullness of joy in that possession. It can know no change; though he can be aware of the changeful world, not as any part or aspect of himself but as his self-created Other. His being includes no conflict; all conflict is outside him, in the Other; though he can have in his own mode a full understanding of all conflicts and a full possession of their resolution, which so often never comes to us in this world.

In this still self-possession and self-enjoyment there is no thinking as we know thinking. He has not our experience of rising above sensibility to intellectual apprehension, for he has no sensibility and no intellect either, if we mean by intellect what it is in us, a faculty of abstraction. Only a single intuitive and yet perfectly explicit apprehension of the total being of the object, which again is not an object in the sense in which things are objects to us. So, and only so, can we dimly hint what existence is for God, what it is to him to be himself.

MAN'S INVOLVEMENT WITH FINITE BEING

The human mind has a continual hunger for being. Receptive by nature, it is like an empty form that is avid of content, and the content has to come from the things which exist around us. The richer their own content, the more they offer for apprehension and appreciation, the more eager our mind is to find and keep on finding them.

The hunger shows itself in early childhood. One can observe the uninhibited experimentalism of children, their eagerness to explore the appearances and qualities and practical potentialities of things, regardless of their elders' preoccupation with cleanliness and safety. Those of us who have a vivid memory of those early years can recall the unaffected delight in colours and sounds, feels and smells, surfaces and textures, the sound of running streams, the gleam of light on wet surfaces, the smell of stone and soil and timber, the feel of metals – the list is infinite. There is joy too in one's active commerce with these things, the yielding natures of some substances and the stubbornness of others, the pleasures of being able to mould or even destroy some things, and the feeling of assurance in the reliability of others. I remember my astonishment at the discovery that older people seemed not to perceive these things and not to want to know; for this was being, this was the warp and woof of the world, and what could be more important than that?

When with greater sophistication one comes to scientific study a more subjective element may enter in, a delight in the exercise of one's own powers, a joy in the achievement of discovery. But the sense of the object is not lost. It is even enriched as we come to find wider connections and more deep-seated structures. Even when scientific theory takes us into a world where the senses and the imagination cannot follow, we still feel that here, though now in an abstract and purely schematic way, we are tracing the rhythms of the things which are.

When we come to knowledge of human beings, such as we have in our every-day contacts with one another and in our reading of histories and biographies, an important frontier is passed. The minds and souls of men are not, like their bodies, presented to any of our senses, nor are they inferred in the way of a scientific theory. We learn about them in a different way, but we do learn, and human life would be very different from what it is if we had not the knowledge which we in fact possess of one another's thoughts and feelings. And here is a new kind of intimacy in knowledge. Human beings are of course among those things which are, and in knowing them we are having knowledge of being; but now for the first time it is knowledge from within. We know what it is like to be a self-conscious personality; we know not merely that other people have certain experiences, but we know what the having of such experiences is like for those who have them. Here is not merely a knowledge, but a quasi-sharing of being by way of understanding and sympathy. Further, those human beings whom we know also know one another and interact with one another, and we understand these interactions too. We can follow, and be in a manner drawn into, their loves and hates, their friendships and their quarrels, their controversies and their dramatic confrontations, which are the stuff of history. We are drawn into the great tides of being, and our own being is enriched thereby.

Furthermore, the respect which we feel for sensible things, simply because they are, rises here to a wholly different plane in the respect which we feel for intelligent personality. One hears of this 'respect' most commonly in connection with a certain moral theory, where it is associated with abstract universal principles. In real life, however, it pervades our emotional and volitional life and shapes our attitudes to one another in all phases of human coexistence. Love, friendship, loyalty, admiration, patience, compassion, none of these would be what they are at their best without this component. It binds us to other people and leads us to make their concerns our own. It brings us into a deep involvement with our fellow human beings, not merely as objects by the contemplation of which our own being is enriched, but as the Other Self in the Not-Self, by our commitment to which our limited selfhood is widened and transcended.

From this continual confrontation with the Self in the Not-Self, in historical and social relationships and in moral commitment, comes the peculiar fascination which we find in human personality. There is a dialectic of likeness and unlikeness, of the intimate and the alien. We can be at home with another human being as with no other created thing; but we can also meet in him an abyss of otherness. It is perhaps a matter of shifting perspectives. Consider the human being as he exists in the physical world. He is conditioned in all his life and thought and action by what surrounds him in that world; yet he also in a sense contains the world in himself by way of consciousness.

This second-order world, this world-reflected-in-a-human-mind, is no mere phantom. It is this, and not the world in its independent reality, which enters into the motives and purposes of the human agent, and it is this that we have to grasp on all those numerous occasions when we need to know not how things seems to us, but how they seem to someone else. All serious discourse is liable to bring us up before this demand. A human self, merely by existing and communicating with us, brings into our range a fresh distinctively slanted vision of the world; to understand someone else is an exercise in changing standpoints, in shifting landmarks, and that is a kind of self-transcendence.

Not only can the human self thus create its own standpoint and its own vision of things, but it can reflect upon itself, making its own thoughts and feelings and purposes an object of knowledge and judgment. It is capable of self-assessment, self-transformation, self-transcendence. And I who am trying to understand the other self must remember that it is a self-transforming being that I am trying to grasp. However far, however deep my understanding goes, the other may always move on and leave me behind.

These strange powers, which I find in other selves around me, I know that I too possess. I am one of them, and each of them is to me an *alter ego*. But there is a tension between the words of this phrase. The other is to me another *self*; I am at home with him, can understand him and be understood, find myself reflected and reaffirmed in him. But he is *another* self; he is different from me, and tomorrow he may be different from his own present self, and to open myself to him is to allow myself to be led beyond myself and my world. It is here, in this dialectic of same and other, this perpetual shifting of perspectives, this experience of being all the time both affirmed and challenged by the other – it is here that the mystery and fascination of human personality reside.

So far our contacts with existing things and people and the building up of our attitudes towards them. But beyond this the creative imagination comes into play. It clothes the objects of our experience with a fresh significance by reflecting our feelings into them and making them symbols of the things which we fear or desire. Thus the objective world becomes a great screen upon which the drives and tensions of our inner life are projected. At the same time we create for ourselves a whole new world of objects – works of art – whose significance lies in their being an objectification in expressive forms of our subjective experience. We are thus set over against ourselves and made to confront ourselves as an undeniable reality. The face of our own self looks back at us out of the not-self.

Throughout this aesthetic realm of experience there runs a dialectic of self and not-self, subject and object. To perceive an object aesthetically involves seeing a structure in it, and very often this structure is not the one which a pragmatically or scientifically motivated perception would select for emphasis. Hence a representation of an object as an artist sees it often appears to the man of common sense to be a wanton distortion. The artist is in fact exploring and reporting on the formal fertility of being beyond the limits set by common sense to our recognition of it. But besides the formal structures which are to be detected in actual experience, the artist also invents new ones of his own, often though not always using natural forms as a taking-off point for his adventures, and here too he is an explorer—exploring the possibilities of form beyond all that is actual in nature. Here objective fact and human invention play box and cox with one another, the human mind scrutinising the forms of nature and making its own variations on them, or working out its own inventions and giving them physical reality. And further, since all formal structures have for us a feeling-value, and complex structures can bear a complex tissue of subtly interwoven feeling-values, the artist in exploring the possibilities of form is also exploring the possibilities of feeling, discovering feeling-value in actual forms and projecting feelings outwards into expressive structures.

From this intimate interplay of art and nature arises sometimes the illusion that the artist discerns a 'deeper reality' in nature, to which the rest of us are blind. Aesthetic theories have arisen which gave a metaphysical significance to 'the beautiful'. Such theories cannot nowadays command credence. The tendency now is to dwell mainly or exclusively upon the expressive value of the aesthetic imagination, its place in the total functioning of the human mind. But it is here as it is with science; while an immense human effort is put forth and a great display is made of human skill, yet the mind does all this in dialogue with nature, and the ultimate outcome of their dialogue is an enrichment of our feeling for the objective world, the world of being.

MAN'S INVOLVEMENT WITH THE INFINITE

When we pass to the religious sphere, to the vision of the All-Agent and all that grows from it, the objective aspect of experience is again dominant. God is the object in and behind all objects. He is not merely someone who is, but Being itself, utter fullness in his own being and the source of all finite beings. Yet at the same time he has a fuller and deeper significance for us than any finite thing, inasmuch as our involvement with him is fuller and deeper than with them. All the relations that we have with them are also relations with him, since at the heart of the being of each of them is he, and besides what they are in themselves they are also incidents in the great game of hide and seek which he is all the time playing with us. In the strength of their being we feel the strength of his. In their claim upon our regard we sense the reflection of his illimitable claim. The whole order of things and the whole sequence of events is the medium of our commerce with him. As his servants, friends and lovers our contact with him is deeper and fuller and more continuous than with any human being. It has also a more thorough transforming influence upon us, leading us (when we will let it) beyond familiar patterns of life and thought into the unknown.

God has the same fascination for us as finite persons have, and for the same reason, the dialectic of likeness and unlikeness in our relations with him. As intelligent beings we are his kin. In him we find our own nature archetypally set forth, and are happy to think ourselves made in his image. But in him we also find ourselves immeasurably transcended. He is immeasurably beyond intelligence as we know it and personality as we exemplify it. Hence on our part an attitude towards him compounded of fear and joy– fear at being so far transcended that we feel ourselves negated, reduced to insignificance and almost to nothing; joy at finding that what is negated in us is reaffirmed in him with an absoluteness of which we are not remotely capable. It is the complex emotion of awe which Otto describes in *Das Heilige*; in fact, God as absolute being is the supreme and ultimate numinous object. He overwhelms, he overawes, he fascinates, he terrifies.

Notable among the attributes which Otto ascribes to the numinous is that of being wholly other (*das ganz Andere*). Much – too much – has been said about this aspect of the numinous; for of course the attribution cannot be true. If it were true, the object would not be attractive to us, nor should we regard it with reverence. It would be to us a sheer blank. God is in fact apprehended as the Like which is unlike, the Unlike which is like, the Near which is unapproachable and the Unapproachable which is near, and in this perpetual tension of attributes lies the characteristic pattern of God-seeing. Otto himself is aware of this. He quotes a passage from St Augustine's *Confessions* in which it is expressed with lapidary clarity: *Quid est illud quod interlucet mihi et percutit cor meum sine laesione? Et inhorresco et inardesco. Inhorresco in quantum dissimilis ei sum. Inardesco in quantum similis ei sum*. We are like him, he is like us, and we speak of him in terms of personal attributes, though we know if we reflect that such terms cannot properly describe him. And he is unlike us, and we take refuge in the impersonal language of ontology and call him being, cause, absolute and the like. But to those who have not the God-vision, and who take the words we use in their generally understood rational sense, both sets of terms will seem flat and empty. They mean something which they cannot properly say. They mean *ipsum esse*, the absolute, the numinous.

If being is an object of hunger to us, it is a hunger which only absolute and infinite being could satisfy; and in fact an aspiration towards the transcendence of finitude and the attainment in some sense of infinity is built into our nature. It shows itself in the romantic dreams of youth, and in the inordinate fantasies and ambitions of later life, as a desire to achieve a kind of infinity or absoluteness in our own being; infinity by experiencing and knowing everything that there is to experience and know, absoluteness in the sense of immunity from weakness and error and all strokes of fate. But even human ambition sometimes deviates into sense, and in our saner moments we know that our only plausible hope of attaining to any kind of infinity or absoluteness is to be united with and energised by the real Infinite, the real Absolute. If that could be, a life beyond our nature and beyond our conception might be realised in us.

For our nature, finite yet insatiable in its longings, bears in itself this paradox, that it can fulfil itself only by going beyond itself. That of course would have to be in another life than this, and it is to the positive religions that we must look for traces of a doctrine concerning it. So in the Mahayana the Buddha, who has achieved total enlightenment and freedom from all the bonds of finite being and all attachments to it, is sometimes referred to as the Well-gone; and Sakyamuni is reported to have said, when questioned as to the state of such a one when he has passed into complete and final nirvana, that it would be misleading to say that he is or that he is not, or both, or neither; nothing that we could say would do justice to the truth. And in the Christian tradition God, who is absolute being, is for that very reason no definite kind of being, for definite entails finite, but is beyond definition or description, *huperousios*, beyond being itself, *pantón epekeina*, away beyond everything as St Gregory Nazianzen sings. And his friend St Gregory of Nyssa, speaking of the consummation of the soul's quest, finds it not in a static condition of contemplative repose, but in a reaching-out, *epektasis*, whereby the soul in union with the Infinite moves in a perpetually renewed exploration of what that union can mean for it.

11 Shifting Perspectives

Our examination of religious experience has reinforced the outlines of our theist truth-model. Those experiences which the experient is apt to describe as perceptions or quasi-perceptions of divine presence and activity turn out to include nothing which an uncommitted observer could accept as empirical evidence for any definite conclusion; though to one who already believes they naturally appear as confirmatory evidence, and for one already inclining towards belief the report of them may serve to clinch his assent. On a broader view, the very existence of this wide world of religious experience is certainly a strong motive inclining towards belief; for the theist mind, as we said, regards it as a sign of the truth of theism that it is coherent and meaningful, and the more one sees of its experiential working-out, the more one has to acknowledge how coherent and meaningful it is. One point we see now which we did not see before, namely that its meaningfulness is not just a static meaningfulness, but something dynamic. The soul advances from stage to stage in a process which is variously described as a pilgrim's journey, or as the ascent of a mountain, or as the climbing of a ladder. If belief in God opens up the possibility of such a progression, and motivates and empowers and directs it, then it may seem that God-belief is not merely a speculative theory, but commands deep secrets of life itself.

The way of ascent as I have described it is a way of increasing intimacy and involvement, a way of union. I wrote the greater part of the previous chapter in a somewhat lyrical tone, expressive of the metaphysical passion with which the soul pursues freedom in the Beyond. But not everyone feels this passion in its full intensity, and no one feels it so all the time. And in one's less exalted moments a different aspect of experience asserts itself: the aspect of habitual affirmations, customary verbal formulae, accepted doctrines and theories, and the restless play of mind upon all these. Here is another path to follow, another ascent to make, another labour to perform. It is the labour of understanding and interpretation, as the mind tries over the years to formulate fully and precisely to itself the content of its beliefs. True, in the end it will be seen that what we mean is beyond anything that we could ever say. But if we told ourselves that at the outset we should not even understand it properly, it would be an *ignava ratio*, a refusal to pay the price of true understanding. That price is the unremitting labour of trying to understand, of turning our images and concepts inside out and upside down, and so learning how little of what we originally said we really meant.

This progression is not usually part of what people have in mind in speaking of religious experience; but it ought to be included if our account of religious experience is to be a balanced one. For it is an integral part of the soul's life as it moves forward, and some of the commonest and most forbidding obstacles occur here.

People professing the same religious belief may differ widely in their understanding of it. Differences occur between persons in the same religious community, and between one period and another in the life of one person. One person will differ from others for reasons which lie in his experience, the manner and context in which the religion has been presented to him, or the extent to which he is equipped to analyse and interpret such things. An individual will differ from himself as a result of growing up, as a result of increasing maturity in the understanding of theism itself and in the adjustment which he makes between it and his other beliefs. At any given time, the believing community will include individuals who are at all stages of personal development, exemplifying all degrees of insight and commitment. A long way back, in Chapter 3, I pointed to the inherent flexibility of theological language and symbolism which makes this variety and continuing development possible. At that stage it was no more than a curious observation arising out of a philosophical puzzle; but at the stage where we now are, it can be seen as an inevitable feature of human thought and expression when their object is 'God'.

THE GROWTH-PATTERN OF GOD-BELIEF

Most people probably make the acquaintance of the God-concept in the context of some religion; and not in the most developed form of that religion, but in the form in which it is apprehended by its ordinary adherents and by outside observers. Thus they will be more familiar with its imagery than with its technical concepts, more at home with its mythology than with its dogmatics. From such a starting-point they may or may not progress to a more critical attitude to current teaching and a more sophisticated concept of God.

It is a law of the human mind in every sphere of discourse that it begins with image-thinking and progresses from that to conceptual thinking and critical analysis. This process in the sphere of God-discourse shows one or two peculiar features.

(a) Since God is not a perceptible object, our initial concept of him cannot be directly derived from perception as are our concepts of empirical objects, but it is constructed by selecting and combining elements from the empirical world. Since the construction is not subject to any control by perception, the mind has great freedom in the choice and combination of its material, and so the forms in which God is represented and the terms in which he is spoken of show considerable variety. It is only fair to add that, as thought progresses, the concept of divine personality begins to act as a kind of control, and what we say about God is increasingly determined by our endeavour to give expression to that.

(b) Because no research can be done upon God as it can upon perceptible objects, and no mathematical formula can be worked out for his nature as it can for the ultimate constituents of matter, image-thinking continues in this sphere far on into the stage of ordered reflection and theological systematisation. Popular belief never breaks free from it, and even trained theologians in their public worship and private devotions continue to use the accepted imagery. Systematic theology itself never escapes into a purely conceptual mode. Some of the long-continuing controversies in theology could not have continued if men had taken seriously the nature of the language they were using.

(c) On the other hand, when the mind has been well exercised in reflection, and begins to turn its attention less upon peripheral matters and more upon God himself, then his absoluteness, completely transcending all finite things, comes to the fore, and we see that all attempts at systematic conceptualisation must fall immeasurably far short of the truth. Darkness is the truest light we get on God, and silence is the best expression of the inconceivable. It is hard to adjust oneself to this truth, nor do we in fact retreat into silence and stay there, for it is necessary to think and speak of God even though we cannot do it adequately; and in fact an adjustment is arrived at. We continue to use our images and concepts, but with an awareness that the real truth is not in them. As our experience of living towards God grows we think of the myths and doctrines less as a description of something which exists and more as a cipher for experiences and for our way forward. Our experience is one of holding commerce with a reality, but a reality which is not known and cannot be known except in this way. We do not know what God is like, but we know how to live with him; and our understanding of him, such as it is, is all in the living.

Much has been said in recent years from a psychological point of view about the way in which 'God' should be presented to children. They cannot, we are told, understand the qualifications with which our language about God needs to be taken; they are at the mercy of a literalism which will have to be paid for in intellectual disturbance when they grow up. Nor are they able in their tender years to understand the deeper aspects of experience which play such a great part in what we say about God; for that reason too they will be forced back upon cruder interpretations of our teaching. My only comment on these contentions is to ask why they should be supposed to apply only to children. It seems to me that they apply in some degree to all God-believers throughout their lives. They are not facts about the child mind, but about God-discourse at all times of life. The only maturity in this field is to know oneself always immature.

If we assume, as a theist in the great tradition would, that the line of development here indicated is natural and normal in a believer, we must also recognise how easily one may fail to follow it through. The possibility of failure is inherent in the very nature of the movement, and that in two ways. Both are essentially forms of inertia.

(a) After going some distance along the road, the traveller may come to a point where he has not the imagination to see what further ground remains to be trodden, and may settle down contentedly with what he already has. Or again, he may *refuse* to see further, because he fears to lose what he already has for the sake of he knows not what. In either case he will become fixated at a point which will be his limit of advance. An example would be someone who lives contentedly in the mythology of his religion and never subjects the imagery to analysis and critical interpretation, either because he has never seen the need, or because in critical questioning he can see nothing but doubt and insecurity. Or take the man who has learned to conceptualise his beliefs and has found a home in a systematic theology such as that of St Thomas. He may resist the discovery of the inadequacy of all such conceptual schemes. St Thomas in his last days declared that all his writings were but straw in comparison with what it had been granted to him now to see. And in our own measure all of us who have risen to the conceptual level in our God-thinking may one day be required to face this realisation, which may come as a slowly dawning conviction or as a sudden insight; and we may resist the disturbing truth and refuse to move out into the Incomprehensibility.

(b) Or one may take the dialectic out of the process by accepting the negations as absolute and failing to see beyond to the reaffirmations. So when an image or symbol is transcended it is quite simply seen as false, and when theological formulae in general are seen to be incapable of adequately describing God, the whole theological enterprise is seen as wasted effort. One can then choose whether to say that we can know nothing about God, and call oneself an agnostic, or to say that one believes there is no God; or one may simply fall dumb from perplexity.

THE PATTERN IN THE PUBLIC MIND

A similar dialectic goes on (of course much more slowly) in the collective mind of a whole believing community, and it is liable to similar fixations and discouragements.

A religion at the beginning of its history, or at a time of revival after decline, or when it is preached to new populations which never heard it before, is presented and accepted primarily in its myth-ological form. And at all times and places, in its great festivals the ritual display, the music and poetry, the piling of midrash upon midrash is the means by which its adherents rekindle the flame of their belief and devotion. The grass-roots of God-belief are always there, in a reassertion of the basic God-vision with whatever imaginative elaboration is characteristic of each particular religion. The Christian festival of the Nativity, which as I write this is due to recur in one week's time, is a case in point.

Belief is always returning to its roots and drawing fresh vigour from the return, but it has also to grow and reflect upon itself. So comes the age of the analytical theologians, the thrashing out of debatable points, the great doctrinal controversies. Along with all this there also appears the work of the contemplatives and the gradual crystallisation of a mystical tradition. Mythology, systematic theology, mystical theology – once these three have been established they continue to exist side by side in the life of the community, and all contribute towards its total belief and experience, though the great bulk of the adherents apprehend their beliefs mainly in the mythological mode, and the thought-discipline of the contemplatives is known to very few.

This state of affairs may last for many centuries. It cannot change except when a revolutionary cultural change takes place, affecting large populations, altering their general level of information and their degree of intellectual awareness. Such a change is in progress today, chiefly in those countries whose prevailing theological tradition has been Christian, and Christianity is showing all the symptoms of an intellectual upheaval consequent upon this. The intellectual level of teaching and discussion among its adherents is higher than it was a century ago, higher than it has ever been before, a growing interest is being shown in the contemplative mode of thought, while at the same time we see those who fear change entrenching themselves in inherited positions, and large numbers moving out through bewilderment into negation.

What is going on is strikingly exemplified in the proclamation of the death of 'God'. In a way this is stale news. His demise was announced by many voices with differing emphases in the nineteenth century; but these were outside voices to which the believers of those days would have thought it wrong to listen with an open mind. What is new in the twentieth century is that the same announcement is being made, again with a variety of emphases, by voices from within the Christian community, and the idea has been noted and has become part of the ferment of questioning which is now going on there.

Why is God thought to be dead? What has given that impression? A variety of causes working together in the cultural revolution of our time.

The most general and least specific of them is the newly diffused questioning spirit and awareness of problems, which far outstrips the knowledge of possible solutions. There have always been ambiguities and even apparent contradictions in 'God' and in the relation between God and the universe, as well as in the distinctive doctrines of particular religions. But they were hardly noticed by the great body of believers. A minority of better-informed people saw the problems and found their own solutions, alone or in discussion with one another, but they would have thought it wrong to come into the open and risk 'shaking the faith' of the ordinary believers, who for their part were glad enough to be left unshaken. Modern education has greatly reduced the size of that docile flock, and in their place has raised up a growing body of insistent questioners. Matters are not improved by the fact that some of these people imagine that the problems were unknown before they themselves became aware of them. They neither know nor care that there is a historical background.

Coming to specific problems, we find that much difficulty is felt over the concept of what is called 'a personal God'. God is commonly presented by the God-vision as a quasi-personal agent, and we saw that there are metaphysical arguments in favour of regarding him as possessed of intelligence and intelligent will, i.e. as a person. But we also saw how his ontological infinity makes havoc of that conception in its most obvious sense, and how in the end we come to a kind of conceiving by failing to conceive, a dialectic of affirmation and negation. That is the intellectual solution, and we can now add that it is the experiential solution too. The well-informed believer treats God as one who addresses men and can be addressed by them, and lives on quasi-personal terms with God in all his affairs, while yet knowing all the time that it is with the Mystery that he is dealing. In all his experience, in his active life, in his thought-life, in his dark contemplation, the balance is kept, in a manner which is more easily lived than spoken.

It is no surprise that some believers cling to the personal image of God and pay at most lip-service to the incomprehensibility. Nor that this rigidity gets mistaken for theist orthodoxy and provokes a reaction. One may then identify God with his personal image and reject him in rejecting it, or one may adopt a belief in a real but non-personal Absolute, such as Spinoza offers. There must be many who, having grown up with a strongly personalistic image of God and a literalistic interpretation of their scriptures and of devotional language, have gasped with joy and relief on being told that God is not really their parents or their church minister writ large, but something in a very different dimension of being. Spinoza has performed this service for many in the last couple of centuries. One may then settle down with one's non-personal Absolute for life. It is perfectly possible to possess a vivid intuition of the All-Agency while steadily refusing to recognise 'God' as a legitimate name for what one sees. The nature-vision of Richard Jefferies and other nineteenth-century writers is a case in point. Or it may happen that one discovers how to personalise one's relations with God without literally meaning what one says. This is an art that is caught by example or comes by intuition, and it does not come to all.

Different from the personality issue, but not unrelated to it, is the issue of the relation between God and the universe. One difficulty with the personal idea of God is that it is thought to entail his being separate from and external to the universe as a human person is separate from and external to the things surrounding him. If then God is said to have any influence on the course of events in the world, this is thought of as 'interference' and so as 'arbitrary'. For this reason (among others) petitionary prayer is rejected, because it is thought to involve just this kind of arbitrary interference with the course of nature by an external power. Here again, to rid oneself of this Supernatural Meddler can come as a relief, a liberation; one is set free to come to terms with nature as it is, to learn its ways and one's place in it, without having to look over one's shoulder all the time.

But an external God like this is untrue to the God-vision, for which, while God is not his creatures and they are not he, yet the very being of the creatures is an energy of God. So we react against the externalised God and try to find ways of expressing the intimate relation which really obtains between him and the world. In doing this, however, we may overshoot the mark and use phrases which come too near to identifying God with the world; and then there is a counter-reaction, with charges of 'pantheism' being flung about. Popular writers discuss whether God is 'in' the world or 'out there' beyond it or in the 'depth' under it. More formal theologians write endlessly of the 'transcendence' and 'immanence' of God. In these discussions the key terms 'in' and 'out' and 'depth' and 'trans' are used with a minimum of analysis and definition, which ensures that the procession of mutual misunderstandings and misrepresentations can go on indefinitely.

The dialectical quality of 'God' has been known to some Christians since the earliest centuries, and there are stories of individuals being troubled by a too sudden discovery of it; such as that Egyptian monk in the days of the Origenist controversy who, on being taught the falsity of anthropomorphism, lamented that he was left with nothing to worship. The knowledge of God as the great Darkness has persisted in the Church, but unknown to the great body of believers, who have apprehended God in rites and myths with little suspicion that there was anything beyond these. What is happening now is that with the rapid growth of knowledge, the spread of popular education, and the wide diffusion of a questioning spirit among the people, issues which once concerned only an intellectual minority are being forced upon the attention of a continually widening public. The logical foundations of God-belief are called in question in a world where not only empiricist philosophers, but the whole educated public, takes for granted the scientific truth-model. The language used is called in question because of its figurative character. The true initiate of course takes this in his stride, using the language easily and unselfconsciously. But modern conditions make us self-conscious about it; and when it has to be explained analytically, as is increasingly felt to be necessary, it seems artificial and we shy away from it. And the substance of what is said about God is questioned at many points: not only the kind of being he is, and his relation to the world of experience, but also his relation to morality, his place as a symbol of authority, his significance as prescribing limits to human freedom. These questions are now alive in the minds of a wide public who are ill equipped to make a patient analysis of them or to find stable readjustments. It is not surprising if the result is bewilderment, discouragement and sometimes withdrawal.

It will be interesting to see what happens when the same disturbing influences come to be felt (as they must some day soon) in the Islamic, Hindu and Buddhist worlds.

It would be hasty to conclude from all this that theism is in deadly peril; but it is undergoing a crisis of unconsciousness, or (to adapt a phrase from St John of the Cross) the whole body of believers is experiencing a night of the intellect. A stabilising influence is to be expected from the heirs of the contemplative tradition, who have a *savoir-faire* in such matters, and from the slow growth of a comparable *savoir-faire* in the more sensitive members of the wider public. In the end a new, less literalistic understanding of language and symbols may be expected to become normal, by virtue of that inherent flexibility of theological expressions upon which the continuing life of theist systems depends.

12 Faith and Commitment

Recent discussion in philosophy of religion has moved on beyond the stage which is reflected in Chapters 2 and 3 of this book. It is accepted that the empiricists have made their point, but it is also accepted that that is not the end of the matter. If theology fails so catastrophically to be empirically grounded factual knowledge, can we be sure that that is what it is trying to be? Can we be sure that it is not succeeding in being something else instead? But then what is it that theology tries to be, and perhaps succeeds in being?

There is a tendency to argue thus: 'Since theology is not knowledge of existing fact, it cannot be intended as reality-assertion.' One then tries to think what it can be. Can it be the telling of edifying stories, or perhaps a recommendation to think and live *as if* what it says were true?

But theologians know quite well when they are telling edifying stories, and their assertion of the existence of God is not one of them. Nor is there any as-if about it. One does not react to an as-if in the way that genuine believers react to God. No, the fact is that theology *is* reality-assertion, and the question we should be asking is: 'What kind of act can reality-assertion be, when it has no adequate grounding either in empirical evidence or in the metaphysical speculations to which its defenders sometimes appeal?'

Both believers and uncommitted observers often call it 'faith', and in the end I shall agree with them; but not before discussing how the word is to be understood, for it is not unambiguous.

In the first place, it does not mean believing on authority. Belief on authority does occur in religion of course, but the authority is always supposed to be ultimately God's, mediated to us through a variety of spokesmen. These spokesmen have authority only in so far as God is believed to speak through them; the acknowledgement of their authority therefore presupposes the acknowledgement of God's existence; and so the acknowledgement of God's existence cannot in turn rest upon their authority. It is a decision which everyone must make for himself in the exercise of his own judgment, as a responsible act.

In what sense is the decision to acknowledge God's existence a 'responsible' act? In the sense that the believer knows he is liable to be called upon to give an account of his decision, and that he is in principle able and willing to give reasons in explanation and defence of it. To say that he is liable to be called to account for his decision is merely to acknowledge that it is a decision from which it is possible to dissent. If dissent is possible, then to decide either way is to take a side, and he who does so may fairly be asked to explain why he thinks it right to take the side he does. He does not know for certain that the view which he has adopted is true, but he is sure that it is the right view to take; and we may ask what makes him so sure.

But 'sure'? Here again a question may be asked. For it is widely assumed that faith connotes uncertainty. It is supposed to mean committing oneself to a belief although one cannot be sure that it is true. One does this apparently through sentimental attachment to the belief, or from some other irrational cause; and this (they say) is an unstable frame of mind, always in danger of being overthrown by some insight into the real state of the case. That is why believers sometimes talk of doubt as an ever-present temptation and exhort one another to resist it.

But on the other hand, faith sometimes seems to display a considerable firmness. It can inspire laborious lives; it can lead believers to face suffering and death rather than deny their beliefs; it has even been known occasionally to survive modern techniques of brain-washing. But of course the determination with which people cling to their beliefs is not necessarily a function of the rationality of the grounds on which they hold them. However subjectively convinced they may be, are there objective grounds which can justify them in being so sure?

Well, if by 'being sure' is meant the possession of logical certitude, then of course God-belief is not an instance of it. Nor is any persuasion relative to existing things, not even the best-supported scientific conclusions. To all of these, if we are to be fully explicit, we must add the qualification: 'but of course this may be wrong'. And yet there is a kind of being sure in science, only it is not a being sure that things are exactly as our theory asserts. It is a being sure that our theory is what the evidence so far available to us indicates. We cannot be sure that our theories are *true* in relation to a supposed independent reality, but we are sure that they are *right* in relation to the evidence. Now, is the God-believer sure of his position in this way? Does he really find that his evidence is such as to constrain assent, or does some other factor enter in?

I am not here speaking of the superstitious believer, or of the intellectually short-winded. No doubt these types are always with us. But I am supposing a believer who is intelligent, serious and well-informed. Now, such a one is certainly in a different position from the scientific believer, because he is aware of the existence of a widely accepted and strongly argued case against theism. He knows that this case can be answered, but never refuted. And therefore, for him, believing means risking a judgment.

This does not mean that he keeps on halting between two opinions. He is sure that the side he takes is the right side; and not merely that it is the right side for him to take, for some personal reason or other, but quite simply that it is *the right side to take*. The non-theist no doubt does not see it so, but that is how it appears to the theist.

Why this difference? Is it because the theist notices relevant considerations which the non-theist overlooks? A believer once said, 'The unbeliever is always talking about something else', meaning that he never sees the point. But what could these other considerations be? Not reasons in the ordinary sense; for we know that all the believer's reasons together do not add up to what would satisfy scientific standards. But in that case we must face the obvious fact: the theist has a ground of conviction which is all his own. Nor can there be much doubt what this ground of conviction is. He believes what he believes because, besides being self-consistent and not flatly contradicted by facts, it can be worked out as a life-pattern in a way which opens up wide possibilities for the satisfaction of the metaphysical passion, the soul's hunger for being. He thinks that is a reason for accepting what is after all a metaphysical, not an empirical, proposition.

And if that is what sways the believer, then to believe is not merely to adopt an opinion or a proposition or a theory. It is to commit oneself to a process of growth and of what may prove to be quite radical change. There is a name for this kind of thinking and this kind of commitment. It is 'existential' thinking, and to assert God is to take up an existential stance.

The truth is that believing in God, taken together with all the consequences which flow from the belief and the possibilities of exploration and discovery which we have seen it opens up, is not analogous to adopting a particular scientific theory; it is analogous to adopting the scientific way of thought with all its principles and possibilities. That too has a transforming effect on mind and outlook, and that too is an existential attitude. There is no *scientific* reason for thinking scientifically; the determination to do so is an existential determination, an acceptance of certain methods and principles because of what they promise to do, and can in part be seen to be doing, to change the quality of human life. Loyalty to science has its confessors and its martyrs just as God-belief has, and the nature of their commitment, in so far as they understand their own action, is the same. A scientist who suffers rather than deny his principles does not suffer for a particular theory, which he must know is subject to criticism and correction; he suffers for the free play of scientific thought, for the freedom to think, even to think erroneously, acknowledging no right of correction in any authority save that of a subsequent more thorough scientific investigation. His commitment is not to a particular set of views, but to the continuing process of research whose ultimate findings he cannot foresee. So likewise the God-believer who suffers for his belief is suffering not for the views which he happens at that moment consciously to hold, but for the right to be involved in that unending quest which is the Godward life. His commitment is to the open-ended process of transformation whose early stages he has already passed, but whose end is beyond conception. And this commitment is the true meaning of 'faith'.

Part IV
BEHIND BELIEF
AND NON-BELIEF

13 *Credo Ut Fiam*

It is time to take stock of our position. What have we so far established? What further questions arise?

THE NATURE AND MOTIVE OF THEOLOGICAL ASSENT

We have found that the reality of 'God' cannot be established by the kind of reasoning which we employ in searching out matters of fact in the empirical universe. Indeed, it is not typical of theist reasoners even to attempt this. Here or there one finds the odd cosmologist, a master perhaps in his craft but not philosopher enough to understand its limitations, who claims to have performed the feat. For the most part, however, the arguments used by those who argue the existence of God are metaphysical ones, as the concept 'God' is itself a metaphysical one. We have examined these arguments and found that they all rest upon assumptions which cannot be justified either empirically or logically. True, there is also the appeal to religious experience. We saw reason to think that such experience is more various in its forms and is shared by more people than appears at first sight. We noted its convincing power for those in whom it is strong. But it cannot count as evidence, as the logic of inductive science regards evidence; for it cannot be unambiguously described and classified, nor can it be experimentally controlled. Even if we concede that it is a fact of life and an indication of something, it cannot be shown that that something must lie outside the empirical world already known to us.

We need not on that account forbid believers to speak, as they often do, of their 'knowledge' of God. We can understand the special senses in which they use the word. Often, when they speak of 'knowing' God, they do not mean in the strict sense knowing that God exists, but 'knowing', in the sense of having quasi-personal acquaintance with, the God in whom they believe. And sometimes they speak of their belief as 'knowledge' because they feel it has a comparable quality of confidence and conviction in it – which in some instances is true. But it remains true that in the intellectual debates of our time theology is always on the defensive, and that fact speaks for itself. If judged by the generally accepted standard of evidence, the scientific-empiricist standard, theology fails the test.

Yet, inadequately grounded in evidence though they are, theological assertions are made and believed and acted on; and not only on particular occasions, but some people base the whole pattern of their lives upon them.

What is going on here? What determines assent, if it is not the force of evidence? And on what grounds, other than the force of evidence, could it be considered justifiable to yield assent?

The attempt which has failed is the attempt to justify belief in God either on the grounds on which belief in ordinary matters of fact is justified, or on the grounds of metaphysical reasoning. But already in Chapter 5 we recognised that these are not the grounds on which God-belief is originally based. We saw that, prior to argument, there is an imaginative outreach, an intuitive vision of the world in solidarity with an All-Agent who is also the Absolute. Later we saw how human life, seen in this framework, takes on new meanings and reveals new possibilities of experience; and that too reflects back upon God who is the Source and Centre of this world of experience. To the ordinary believer this comprehensive view of things seems inherently convincing. Its unity and its wealth of significance speak for themselves. When he is not under some special pressure to argue a case, he feels that no argument is needed. Though he would not claim to 'see' God as a distinctly perceptible object, he does 'see' the God-centred unity of all existence as the obvious truth about all existence. It does not occur to him that he himself might have invented all this, that it might be a projection of his own mind; he would not credit himself with the resources for such a construction. And if he has not himself constructed it, it must be that he sees it because it is there to be seen.

But the God-vision is not alone in the mind. It has to coexist with critical reflection of one sort or another. Even comparatively unsophisticated people make observations, and ask questions, which have a bearing on the God-centred vision of things. The ambiguity of so much that is said about God, the variety of doctrines and practices, the all-pervading evil of the world and the failure of prayer and godliness to avert suffering – these things need no theoretical elaboration, the simplest can see how they raise doubts against the truth of the God-vision. It is an old question which arises anew for each generation: shall we go on believing, or not?

And old as is the question, so also is the answer which the believing consciousness gives. It does not take the form of a theoretical argument such as those whose inconclusiveness we have seen. They belong to an advanced stage of sophistication which not everyone, even in these days, attains. The native language of the believing mind is different from all that. It talks of God not as an entity whose existence may be discussed in the abstract, but always in solidarity with the life-pattern which results from the acknowledgement of his existence. The theist offers us not a proposition or a theory, but a life. The belief in God, the emotional responses and the patterns of behaviour are all parts of one package deal and are offered for our acceptance *en bloc*. That this is the believer's approach is manifest everywhere in the literature of religious edification, apologetic and propaganda. To believe as against not believing is not to adopt an opinion, but to embrace a life. It is the same in the controversies over the relative merits of different religious systems; they are judged not as thought-systems but as life-systems. A Christian will argue the superiority of his religion to Buddhism, for example, in terms of the kind of life and character which they respectively produce, and the Buddhist replies in kind.

This is the real inner dynamic of God-belief. It is so in the simplest believing mind, and it remains so however far learning and critical reflection may advance. But of course learning and critical reflection bring with them the urge to elaborate. It was these influences which brought into existence the tradition of metaphysical theology which we have been examining – a sustained attempt to buttress belief by methodical argument from known facts and principles. Yet even in the heyday of that tradition it was recognised to be a thing for the learned. The real ground of faith, for the ordinary believer and even for the learned themselves, was that which we have stated here, the acceptance of a belief in solidarity with a life. And today, when metaphysical theology is discredited and when the spread of scientific ideas has produced a higher level of critical awareness in the public mind than ever before, the inner dynamic of God-belief needs to be more closely examined than it has hitherto been.

The believer accepts not just a doctrine, but a life and a doctrine as belonging together, the doctrine belonging with and being part of the life, and the whole complex self-authenticating. The fact which stands out here is that God-recognition is not a purely or even predominately intellectual act, but is the acceptance of a life-pattern in which the doing of certain things is made possible by, and therefore is inseparable from, the asserting of certain things.

The reader will remember Professor Braithwaite's theory that it can be allowable, nay, right and proper, to make theological assertions for the sake of the life-pattern for which they provide a framework, but that it is not necessary on religious grounds, and may be impossible on scientific and philosophical grounds, to believe these theological assertions to be true. I do not doubt that a kind of religion exists which fits Braithwaite's description, and that an indeterminable number of people profess theological beliefs in a Braithwaitean sense. But there is another kind of religion, centred upon the devotion of the believer to his God and the reciprocity between them, which cannot subsist unless the theological assertions are believed to be true, and God to be a reality. This is the kind of religion concerning which Jung made the disconcerting discovery that it has great therapeutic value, but that it will not work unless the patient believes it, which unhappily some patients cannot do. But the believer is one who can assent to a theological world-scheme because in spite of intellectual difficulties it has a degree of intrinsic plausibility and it calls for a life-pattern in which he finds meaning and satisfaction. He sees other believers, he learns their doctrine and envies their life, he says *sit anima mea sum eis*, and he commits himself to their life-pattern and their world-view.

This idea of accepting a reality-picture in solidarity with a life-pattern, stated thus baldly, will sound odd to some. But it is current in theological and religious circles, and no one there seems to feel any need to apologise for it. More, it used to underlie a great deal of the speculative thinking which was called philosophy; but more of that later.

It raises two issues to which we must now turn our attention: (1) It appears to be a case of asserting objective existence on subjective grounds. Can anything be said in favour of such a practice? (2) If we are offered rival reality-pictures in solidarity with rival life-patterns, is there any way of reaching an argued decision between the contestants?

The remainder of this present chapter will be devoted to the former of these questions.

THINKING TO LIVE

Above, in Chapter 10, I showed how human life is a many-levelled confrontation with objective reality, or with what is believed to be such. For I do not mean the physical interaction which is perpetually going on between the human organism and its environment, but a conscious encounter, to which objective and subjective elements, the existing reality and the human response to it, are alike essential. It is not enough for something to exist; if there is to be a response, it must be recognised as existing. Even a false belief in the existence of something will provoke responses to that something; and conversely, if we are not aware of a thing which really exists, from our point of view it is as if it did not exist, in fact it does not exist for us.

It follows that the world with which the human race has through the centuries been interacting is the world which the human mind has contructed for itself; not the world as it is in itself (if that phrase means anything), nor the world as physical science may now or in the future present it to us, but the world as we from time to time have imagined and imagine it to be, the world as a fact of common experience. And this world has a history, which is part and parcel of the cultural history of mankind. Man makes his world, constructing it from the data which elementary sense-experience offers to him; and through making it and through his responses to it he slowly makes himself. Man and his world grow up together, and neither can be fully understood except in terms of its relation to the other.

Saying this does nothing to impugn the 'independent reality of the object' in any sense which I am able to attach to the phrase. But it emphasises the extent to which what we consciously 'find' in experience is what we have ourselves unconsciously built up.

The ordinary man thinks that in perception he is in direct contact with really existing things, and he is not wrong in this. In so far as we can be said to have such contact with existing things, it is in perception that we have it. But what the ordinary man does not realise is the amount of sheer construction which goes into his perceiving, how much his mind adds to the deliverance of the senses, and how much he takes for granted in doing this. The senses can register only what is here and now, and only those aspects of it which are directly presented to the perceiver. To perceive things as it were in the round requires a great deal of imaginative supplementation. And we do not only perceive things as three-dimensional objects existing in themselves, but as parts of a world. Although the greater part of this world is outside the field of perception at any given moment, we 'know' it is there, and what we perceive here and now is related to innumerable things which we do not perceive here and now, most of which indeed we never shall perceive. As we grow to maturity, more and more information about this surrounding world comes to be stored in our minds in the form of images and concepts. This store of information, based upon perception but extending far beyond it, is what constitutes our every-day knowledge of the real world. In every moment of perception, this body of experience is there as a background, giving context and significance to what we perceive.

Experience is built up by repeated acts of thought, and every such act is performed in a here and now, but it reaches out far beyond what evidence the senses provide in the here and now. It takes for granted that there are other places beyond the here, and that there has been a past and will be a future beyond the now. It takes for granted that memory is a true witness to the past, and that in the future the patterns of things and events will generally be found to resemble those of the past and the present. All our reality-thinking, all our exploration of the universe around us, depends on these assumptions. Although it could not begin without the evidence of the senses, it progresses only by going beyond that evidence, by interpreting it into something vastly more than the senses actually tell us.

No one in his senses is going to suggest that this procedure is wrong, or that the assumptions underlying it are assumptions which ought not to be made. But what precisely are we doing when we make them? What suggests them to us in the first place? How do we *know* that they are right?

As regards their origin, perhaps we ought to refuse to let analysis blind us to the obvious; perhaps we ought to recognise that perception, however many mental functions may have gone into its production, appears full-blown in consciousness as a comprehensive grasp of many details in one pattern, and that there in the specious present we have an elementary experience of duration, and of structures in simultaneity and succession, by extrapolation of which we obtain our explanatory clues for the wider universe. But this extrapolation is always a reaching out beyond the given, beyond the verified, beyond the known. The source of an idea is not necessarily an authority for the use we make of it, and it is an old story in philosophy by now that the guiding principles of our reality-exploration are not logically certain.

Yet no one doubts our right to them, and there is surely no doubt why. We cannot think towards reality on any lines but these. No one can devise any alternative. And without thinking towards reality we cannot act, cannot even live. There is no alternative to this way of thinking except to stop thinking altogether, which means to lie down and die, and this no one will recognise as a real alternative at all. And because there is no real alternative, there is no serious debate, for there is nothing at issue. The principles of our reality-thinking are prejustified (if one may put it so) by the fact that no rival to them can be suggested, and they are massively postjustified by the success which attends their application.

This is a satisfactory authentication of our principles, but it is not an authentication on logical, but on pragmatic, grounds. The whole structure of our reality-thinking is built up on a pragmatic basis. The ordinary man is not explicitly aware of this, but he feels it in his heart, and that is why he is so sure of his (and our) thought-processes. There is no alternative except death, which he will not acknowledge to be a real alternative. His fundamental convictions therefore (and ours) are firmly grounded on the will to live. Behind all theories, behind even the common reason of mankind, the ultimate compelling force is not the intellect, but the will to live.

Religious apologists often see their advantages here. Told as they are on every hand that science is knowledge whereas religion is merely faith, they seize their chance to equalise things by showing that science too, in the last analysis, rests upon nothing better than faith. As they phrase it, in order to think at all, in order to live at all, we have to have faith in our minds and in our working principles; and while it is not suggested that this faith is misplaced, faith is what it is, and not knowledge. If then science, making so vast an act of faith, is so richly rewarded, and the justification of the act of faith lies in the reward, why (they ask) is not the equally far-reaching religious act of faith equally justified by the rewards it brings? The logic is the same for both. They are entitled to equal status and esteem.

Concealed in this argument is a valid point which it must be our business to extricate. But it will be found that the matter is not as simple, and the argument does not tell as definitely in favour of theism, as the apologists think. It is true that the vast difference

between crude sense-experience and the fully developed experience
of intelligent men is all due to the mind's own activity, sifting, co-
ordinating and interpreting the data of sense in accordance with a
variety of working principles. But it is a *variety* of working principles,
they are not all of the same kind, the reasons which justify their use
are diverse, and the truth-status of the results to which they lead is
not always the same.

THOUGHT-PATTERNS AND LIFE-PATTERNS

First, and fundamental to all the rest, is the activity whereby we
spell out and explore the world of ordinary experience, the sensible
world, the world which we all share, through which we know and
communicate with each other. Awareness of and communication
with each other comes very early in the process, and from then on
there is a sharing of experience and information, so that the picture
of the sensible world which emerges in our developed minds is a
communal product, the shared world built up by the shared labour
of innumerable human minds through the centuries, constituting
the richest and most solid block of tradition in our cultural
history.

All this is done by taking principles of structure which are
inherent in our perception of surrounding objects, and extending
them indefinitely beyond the range of possible perception, on the
tacit assumption that we shall then be able to trace the structures of
really existing things. Of course, the picture of the world which is
thus built up keeps changing in detail as exploration reveals more
and more to us; but in its fundamental conceptions common sense is
universal and unchanging. The plain man, however, who is the
creator and upholder of the common-sense world, has no explicit
methodological consciousness of what he is doing, or of the
operations which he performs in doing it. He does it instinctively,
and there is nothing to cause him, so long as he remains a plain man,
to ask any logical or epistemological questions.

Common sense is concerned with the world of existing things, the
world which we see and hear and feel all around us. So too is natural
science, but with such different methods and with such a distinctive
consciousness of aims and principles, that it must be regarded as a
distinct cultural activity and achievement.

Science in its origins had no desire to challenge the received common-sense version of the world, only to see its structures and processes more clearly. From an early date it was seen that progress could best be made if natural phenomena could be expressed in mathematical terms; and when in modern times the method was found of combining mathematical models with experimental checks, progress became very rapid. But at the same time the model of basic physical theory has come to bear less and less resemblance to anything perceptible. Today the world-picture presented by natural science is quite different from that of common sense, constructed of different components by different principles of combination. Yet the two pictures run parallel, and the scientific picture would certainly be wrong if they did not. Every phenomenon in the sensible world can be explained or predicted by calculation within the system of physical theory. And the ordinary man, who at this stage in history has usually some knowledge of scientific conceptions and theories, lives in what may be called a palimpsest world, the abstract characters of his scientific ideas being written on top of, without obliterating, the common-sense ideas which he shares with his pre-scientific ancestors.

Scientists are generally reflective people, and conscious of the principles on which they are working. This work is something more than those exploratory ventures which we have to make in order to live. Science is not merely an exploratory venture, though of course it is that; but it is also a magnificent intellectual construction, a work of art in that sense in which art means skill, and the capacity to perform such a work and the devotion felt to the enterprise give life a different style from what it had before. If anyone asks a justification for the labour of the scientific mind and for the logical venture which that labour entails, the answer is not in terms of our need to think in order to live, but of our resolve to think and live in a certain style. Those who appreciate the scientific life-style think that man would not be fully man without it. It is part of what, to them, is authentic humanity.

But to speak of authentic humanity is to make a normative judgment; and that brings us on to the next stage in our pyramid of concepts, which is built of a different material from reality-statements. It is the stage of value-judgments, norms and precepts.

It is a wide field, which until recent years has not been adequately explored by philosophical analysts. Fortunately I have no need here to try to analyse in detail – only to call attention to a few fairly obvious points.

A value-judgment is not an assertion that anything exists, or that any existing thing is of a stated kind; what it does is to express an attitude, favourable or unfavourable, towards some actual or possible existent. Such an attitude may be very simple and easy to describe, or it may be complex and hard to analyse. In some cases a good deal of reasoning may be involved before the subject's attitude is fixed and ready for expression. But however much reasoning there may be, it is not of the kind which takes place in reality-thinking; and in other cases there is none at all, only an immediate unthinking affective response to some stimulus, such as a pleasant or unpleasant sensory impression.

With this simple and direct kind of value-judgment we are all familiar, and there is nothing much to be said about it. It is the expression of an unthinking response of liking or disliking, and the subject in making this response is not guided by any principle. He is presumably acting in accordance with psychological and physiological laws, but that is a different matter. There is no principle which he can apprehend and apply and so be guided to the appropriate response. He may of course, from the memory of past experiences, frame some generalisations about what he has found his own likes and dislikes to be, but he will not suppose that such a generalisation could have the force of a principle. There are no principles from a prior grasp of which our likes and dislikes in respect of immediate sensory experiences can be derived.

Much more complex and subtle and indeed tantalising is the field of aesthetic judgments, and nowhere perhaps has their inherent mysteriousness been more boldly displayed than in Kant's treatment of them. Anxious as he was to make a systematic analysis which would become part of his comprehensive analysis of the workings of human reason, he was yet determined to be honest about all the difficulties, and the result is that he more than any other writer on the aesthetic judgment has exhibited the paradoxes and tensions in which it is enveloped. It is not a judgment of mere liking, for we notoriously argue about it as we do not about mere sensory pleasures. On the other hand, is it (how can it be?) derived from a principle which we could know and logically apply? Since the eighteenth century the conventional wisdom has been that aesthetic judgment is always intuitive, deriving from inspection of the particular object and not from the application of a principle, and that no principle can in fact be found which could be formulated with enough precision to serve as a premise for aesthetic valuations. I do not contest this, but I call attention to the historical fact that humanity has been loath to believe it. One culture-group after another has expressed its *Kunstwille* in definite principles and channelled the creative and appreciative imagination of its people along the chosen lines, as if in defining its own style of beauty it was defining beauty itself. But even in the ages when definite aesthetic conventions were most in fashion, the creative genius of the artist could bend the rules, and the judgments of the discerning critic came direct from his perceptions and were not deduced from his professed principles. In a word, we have in the phenomenon of aesthetic judgment a fascinating example of man's propensity to seek for absolute value-principles, even in a sphere where he cannot abide by his principles when he has formulated them. It is part of man's desire to organise his life-style. The *Kunstwille* is only one aspect of a *Lebenswille*, a will to live in a certain style; and this will coexists with the creative and exploratory energies of the mind which resist stylisation.

The desire to organise life in a definite style according to recognised principles finds its fullest and most substantial expression in the sphere of morality.

There is great variety here in the kind of language we use and the kind of things we say or do by means of it. There are simple expressions of approval, wherein we declare our favourable judgment upon qualities of character, or upon types of action. These may refer only to a particular instance, or they may be and very often are generalised and become principles declaring that certain qualities of character and certain types of action are always to be approved. We construct ideals, and typical hero-figures embodying these ideals, and use all the powers of persuasion to induce people to strive towards them. Or we lay down precepts, sometimes in the form of proverbial phrases and slogans and sometimes in the form of quasi-legal imperatives, to which we require ourselves and one another to conform. Again we bind ourselves by resolves, vows or other forms of commitment to some particular line of conduct or aspiration. All these, and more besides, constitute the rich fabric of moral discourse.

The moral life, i.e. that complex of activity to which moral discourses is relevant, subsists concretely in the *mores* of social groups. It needs no great skill to discern that these *mores* are the outcome of a variety of shaping influences. Elements of economic advantage or what is believed to be such, elements of class prestige and social solidarity enter in. But there is also unquestionably a degree of feeling for the general good of mankind and for principles which could be valid everywhere and always because they answer to the universal human condition. One such principle which moralists have extricated and formulated is that of aiming at the maximum satisfaction of men's needs and desires and the minimum of deprivation or frustration. Under one form of words or another, this principle has commanded wide acceptance in theory, and has even been effective sometimes as a stimulus to radical reforms in society. Of equal importance with it is the principle of the respect due to intelligent personality, whether in oneself or in anyone else – the principle which in different ways underlies the eudaemonist, the Stoic and the Kantian ethic. By these and similar principles moralists have tried to rationalise existing *mores*, making them as far as possible consistent with what such principles require; and indeed some progress has been made, where the moral consciousness of one age has accepted and partially implemented principles which previous ages did not recognise. However, it is hard to foresee a time when the *mores* of society may be altogether rationalised in this way.

Moral discourse has nothing to do with describing the natural world. It has to do with the construction of man's own world, the world of organised human lives and activities, which man builds up for himself inside nature. This world is the framework in which man realises himself as man. It is the home of authentic humanity. It is the triumph of man's will not merely to live, but to live thus and thus, in what he considers to be a properly human fashion of life. If anyone seeks a justification for the acceptance and enforcement of moral principles, the answer is that this is the precondition for being human as man understands humanity.

THE DISTINCTIVENESS OF GOD-THINKING

Here then, from science through the aesthetic to the moral realm, is a great structure built up by the human mind to house a human life-style. And now, the traditional function or *Sitz im Leben* of God-belief is to crown this structure. It does so by opening up rich possibilities of activity and experience, giving background and deeper meaning to some of the possibilities opened up already in the cultural and moral spheres, and opening up others peculiar to itself.

By making God the centre to which everything is referred, it integrates all thought and experience while at the same time giving man a significant place in the universe.

More in detail, (a) the doctrine that God is an intelligent being, and that intelligence in man is a reflection of the archetypal intelligence which is God's, strengthens the respect which we are in any case disposed to feel for intelligence in human beings, and encourages us in all those activities which develop and display this attribute. These include the moral and social relationships which are possible between intelligent persons. Indeed, there seem to be people who feel that the thought of God comes home to them best when they can see him as the inspirer and patron of personal relationships among men.

(b) A fresh field of personal relationships is opened up, i.e. of relationships with God himself. I showed in Chapter 7 how our relationships with God develop into a dramatic interaction between him and us. And because he is the All-Agent, we meet him in action everywhere, and so an aspect of personal significance is given to events which would otherwise be mere impersonal natural occurrences. The 139th Psalm is a classic expression of this ubiquity of God and the alternating emotional reactions which it can provoke. And again, whereas our contacts with other human beings are necessarily limited and engage only some aspects of our being and activity, our contacts with God are potentially and in principle unlimited, leaving no aspect of our experience untouched and unaffected. As the Psalm already referred to shows, there is a side of our personality which fears such total involvement, but there is also a side, the characteristically religious side, which welcomes it.

(c) But since God is the Absolute, the Infinite, he is to us always the Beyond. Even those things in him with which we seem to be able to find an affinity are in their divine reality quite beyond our compass. To some people this spells frustration; they think it cancels all the positive things we have said. They may even try to evade it by constructing a finite 'God', who to a theist *pur sang* is no God at all. But to others the Beyondness means liberation – liberation from the finite world and from finite human nature itself. For it is part of the mystery of human personality that it recognises its true self-fulfilment only in self-transcendence. Finite as it is, and incapable of becoming anything but finite, it can yet see beyond all finites, including its own finite self; and what it can see beyond, it must needs aspire to transcend. This it finds a way to do by an intimate union with the Infinite, such as a finite being can enjoy without ceasing to be finite: i.e. possessing God always in contemplation, and energised by him in frequent acts of self-transcending vision. This is part of what is meant by the spiritual marriage, the soul's crowning union with God in this life.

Such, seen at their best, are the effects upon life of a standard-type God-belief. It is for the sake of these effects, of the life-pattern which they constitute, that theism asserts the existence of God. One can see how religion queens it over the other human activities to which it gives unity and enhanced significance. One sees how theology queens it over the other sciences; that is, if theology is a science, a body of well-grounded propositions, at all. But this assertion which theism makes is unique, and uniquely questionable, among the activities of the intelligent mind.

It is not (in spite of the apologists) analogous to the assertion of the reality of the world by common sense, or to the act of faith (if we care to call it so) which underlies that assertion. What impels common sense to its assumptions and its assertions is the will to live, which is basic to all possible human activities and from which no human being not under extraordinary pressure thinks of contracting out. And what the 'faith' of common sense (or for that matter of science) gives us is only the formal possibility of a world of experience, the possibility of exploration and experimentation, leaving open the question, what kind of world our explorations and experimentations will disclose to us. But what impels theism is the will to live a particular kind of life which some people think to be outstandingly rich and meaningful; and for the sake of that it ventures upon a vast reality-assertion whose inherent obscurity and dialectical character should by now be quite clear to us. Furthermore, common sense is massively verified by the entire experience of the entire human race. Science is verified by the experience of all the people throughout the world who have mastered its methods and applied them. It is so well verified that it serves as the very model of what verification should be. But theism is 'verified' only by the experiences of some adherents, which large numbers of people do not share and do not understand. In the one case it is the will and experience of all humanity, and in the other it is only the will and experience of a special group.

Nor of course is theism analogous to the enunciation of moral and other principles; for in enunciating them no reality-assertion at all is made.

Theism in short stands alone in making reality-assertions in order to house a life-pattern which not all men desire, with the support of evidences which neither a robust common sense nor science would take seriously as a basis for such an assertion.

MYTHOLOGY, METAPHYSICS AND THEISM

Logically theism stands alone; but in another sense it is not alone, for it is one instance among others of a widespread tendency to tie in a life-pattern with a world-picture, treating the life-pattern as in some way derivative from the world-picture. Such is the age-long shape of philosophy; not of course if by philosophy we mean logical or linguistic analysis linked with an empiricist theory of knowledge, but certainly if we take into account the great long-lived philosophical traditions such as Platonism and Stoicism, and in general what is called the *philosophia perennis*. Philosophies of this type clearly meet, or at least have in the past met, a need felt by others besides philosophical specialists. It is the same need which on a less rational and more figurative level of discourse is met by the construction of a myth.

What do I mean by a myth? In ordinary speech we apply the term to the stories which people tell about their gods, about first and last things and about the order of nature. Such stories are regarded as forming part of people's religion, and we call them myths when they belong to any religion but our own; this exception is due to the fact that in common speech 'mythical' connotes 'false'. Myths play a complex part in the life of the communities in which they are current, but it would be true to say that they express men's beliefs and attitudes with regard to cosmic powers and processes, and also to those psychical and spiritual powers and processes which are determinative for human existence – such as birth and death, youth and age, love, success, suffering. A myth sets forth in figurative expression what a particular community thinks of these things. It tells us, though in dark sayings, why the world and human life in it are as they are, and why our ideals and duties are what they are. To use a hackneyed phrase, it expresses our view on the meaning of life.

A philosophical system does just the same thing, only in a more abstract way. It uses a philosophical terminology, and presents its story as an argued conclusion. Accordingly it is possible in such a system to distinguish three principal components: (a) An account of the nature of the universe, the fundamental principles of the world-order, the ultimate causes of things – in short an ontology or doctrine of being. This is the foundation for what follows. (b) An anthropology, or doctrine of the nature and destiny of man. Is man merely a natural phenomenon, or is he something else as well? What future has the human race amid the impersonal forces of the material world? Has the individual human being a destiny beyond his threescore years and ten? Questions like these are, I believe, the real centre of interest in a philosophical system of the classical type. (c) A life-paradigm, that is to say a model of the kind of intellectual and practical activity which will enable us to get the best out of life in the light of what we believe under (a) and (b). The system as a whole does the work of a myth; or if we prefer we may say it is itself a kind of myth, the kind which a sophisticated society with some intellectual pretensions will be likely to fashion for itself.

From a critical point of view, perhaps the most striking feature of such a system is the passage from (a) and (b) to (c) – from a factual account of the nature of things and of man to a life-paradigm. Here is an attempted synthesis of reality-statements with value-judgments, an attempted passage from the former to the latter. It is a commonplace nowadays that in strict logic there is no passage from any description of things to the judgment that some things are good. But in real life we do tend – yes, all of us, even those who are analytical philosophers – to establish a link between our vision of the existing world and our world of values. How is this done?

(a) A value-judgment is not a descriptive statement; it is the expression of an attitude. But we tend to make our attitudes stable and consistent, to react to similar things in similar ways; and where a coherent character and outlook has been built up, the things to which we react with favourable or unfavourable judgments fall into a coherent system and can be made the object of a value-theory – by which I mean not a theory as to what is meant by calling anything good, but an ordered account of those things which we do in fact call good. Moral theories of the traditional type, which concern themselves with formulating principles from which our detailed moral judgments may be deduced, are all instances of this kind of theory.

(b) There are certain types of things and processes which human beings show a persistent tendency to regard with approval and therefore call good. For example, we feel an instinctive sympathy with life, intelligence, personality – a feeling which finds classic expression in the ethical principle that persons are always to be regarded as ends in themselves. In particular cases the recognition of this principle is often cut across by other motives leading to indifference or hostility, and these counter-motives are very various in their operation. Nevertheless the underlying principle is clearly discernible and is an important fact of human nature.

(c) We like to think that those things which we call good have in some way a central position or a special significance in the universe. There are various ways in which this might be so: a theist world-view offers one of them, a doctrine of progress offers another. Either of these doctrines enables its adherents to feel that in prizing those things which they do prize and embracing the life-pattern which they do embrace they are acting 'in accordance with the nature of things'; and this feeling does much to strengthen their attachment to the life-pattern.

This, then, is what a philosophical system of the classical type is meant to do and does. It paints a picture of the world as having a certain structure, and of man as having certain place in the world-structure; and it points to a certain life-pattern as being somehow 'in accordance with' this world-structure. Or (to put it the other way round) it picks out those aspects of the universe which seem to suggest and encourage a particular way of living, and argues or asserts that these aspects are determinative of the whole. By doing this it gives (for those who can believe it) a sense of direction to life.

It is an essential feature of philosophical systems of this traditional type, that the ontological and the anthropological parts of them are presented as embodying knowledge of reality, knowledge of the nature of things, indeed as a kind of science. And as long as this could be plausibly done there was no logical weakness in the system. Over the centuries, however, the element of logical analysis and criticism in philosophy has come increasingly to the fore. Today it may be said that critical philosophy has criticised the philosophical systems out of existence. Their pretence of logical and metaphysical solidity will not hold, and those who still cling to theism can no longer use that kind of philosophy as an ally. Theism stands alone, alone in that world in which Nietzsche proclaimed a hundred years ago that God is dead.

God as a knowable object, God as the secure point from which we can take our bearings and know that because this is the nature of the real, this must be the meaning of life – that God is indeed dead. If we are to have landmarks and an organised pattern of life, we cannot find them in him. Nietzsche himself had the courage to face the only alternative: if we cannot read off the meaning of life from the nature of things, we must proclaim it by our own legislative act. If we cannot discover that this is the meaning of life, we must proclaim that this *shall be* the meaning of life. It is a bold decision and not without nobility, the decision of man, jerked into maturity by the discovery that he is alone in the world, to take charge of his own destiny and to determine for himself what humanity shall mean. But the man who, in the awareness of the true intellectual situation, still asserts his belief in God, is more subtle and more devious than that. Believing that there can be no satisfactory replacement for God, and inheriting from past ages a technique whereby God's all-sustaining agency can be read in the things of the world and the events of history, believing too that, for him, to be really and fully human depends upon reading the world in that way, he legislates a reality into existence and proclaims 'This is and shall be our reading of experience'.

It is evident how this attitude would stand open to question, even if no rival concept of authentic humanity were in sight. But that is not the case. We must now see how it is challenged by a different reading of experience which provides a model for humanity which needs no ambience of God-agency to house it.

14 The Divided Mind of *Homo Sapiens*

The heyday of metaphysical theology, so far as Europe is concerned, was in the thirteenth century. Immediately afterwards came a change. A keener sense of logical rigour undermined the great scholastic structures, and fifty or a hundred years later strong voices were proclaiming that propositions about God and the soul are matters not of knowledge, but of faith. This did not mean that people had lost their confidence in theism or in Christianity. Faith, though it was not knowledge, was a perfectly respectable and reliable state of mind. This view of the matter became accepted and was later a component in the doctrines of the Reformation.

THE THOUGHT-REVOLUTION OF MODERN TIMES

What really shook the foundations of theism was not the late mediaeval critical philosophy, but the change in natural science which took place about the beginning of the seventeenth century, and which amounted to one of the greatest thought-revolutions in history. At its heart was a new method of investigating nature, a new conception of what questions it was worth while to ask, and an increasingly subtle and powerful technique for finding the answers. In course of time this gave the ordinary educated man a new conception of what thinking could be, which was also a new ideal of what thinking should be. At the same time the application of the new method led gradually to a new world-picture. On the broadest scale, in cosmology, and the narrowest, in the analysis of the structure of matter, the world revealed itself to be very different from what had been generally supposed. So too did man's nature and position in the world, his origin and possible destiny.

The first and second components of the traditional metaphysic being thus transformed, so also was the third. With changed conceptions of himself and of everything around him, man took up changed attitudes, new hopes and aspirations, new value-judgments and working principles, in fact a whole new culture. And this culture, shaped as it was by the development of the scientific mind and scientific discovery, incorporated in itself an expectation of being continually reshaped by the further action of the same causes. This reshaping, confidently expected, was welcomed as a good thing and was called progress. Civilisation became for the first time progress-oriented.

It was natural that this new science-minded culture should generate a myth to express in simple popular terms what it thought of itself, especially of its origins and its future destiny. This myth was the myth of Reason, one of the most widespread and most influential of all the myths of the modern world.

But what is meant here by 'reason', and wherein lies the 'myth'?

Etymologically reason = *ratio* and is equivalent to *logos*. The earliest use of this word to signify a human capacity was that in which it meant the power of reasoning or ratiocination, the power of logical discourse, the power to assemble considerations and evidences and draw conclusions from them. It is a capacity without which man would not be man, for it is only by its exercise that we obtain information about the surrounding world, and are able to foresee consequences and so to plan and act (as we say) rationally.

On the other hand *ratio* itself would be useless if it were the only thought-function we could perform. Equally necessary is the capacity to grasp a complex of related terms intuitively, in a single glance, as constituting a whole. It would do us no good to explore relations and dependences piecemeal, discursively, if we could not intuitively grasp the field of enquiry before we begin and the shape of our discoveries when we have finished. This capacity for grasping a structured whole is called in Latin *intellectus* and in Greek *nous*; the English equivalent is often 'understanding'. *Intellectus* and *ratio*, mutually dependent and playing into one another's hands, together constitute the thinking capacity of man.

In all three languages, Greek and Latin and English, the word 'reason' or its equivalent is often used to mean both together. It is thus when for example we hear questions about reason and faith, or reason and revelation, or reason and emotion, or the length to which reason can go towards obtaining knowledge of God. In all such contexts reason means the thinking mind, the mind in the exercise of all its thinking powers, and not just *ratio* in the narrow sense.

But reason also means more than the simple capacity for reasoning, or for thinking in general. It means that capacity used to its full potential, i.e. not just thinking, but systematic, methodical, self-critical thinking – to a modern speaker, of course, scientific thinking; and it means a habit of mind which sets a high value on such thinking. Reason in this sense is an important cultural and historical force. It leads to discovery and to progress in discovery of truth. It leads to the growth of what is called enlightenment; nay, in a truer sense it is itself the essence of enlightenment, sc. not the actual knowledge to which the exercise of reason leads, but the reason-loving, enquiring, open-minded spirit which expresses itself in the exercise of reason. It is in this sense that we can speak of an Age of Reason or of Enlightenment, meaning the age when the spirit of enlightenment came to be more widely understood and shared than it had been before.

The myth of Reason, to which I alluded above, is concerned with reason in this last sense. It is the core of a dramatic story which tells us how man has become what he now is, and what he may yet become. Man was not man at all before he became capable of thought, at least on that level of efficiency which is represented by common sense. He did not become mature as man until he became capable of fully rational, i.e. scientific, thinking. This happened only in modern times; and so the greater part of past history is the story of man slowly making his way through the ignorance and incapacity, the empty dreams and fantasies of childhood to the moment of maturity. On the way he has had, like Bunyan's pilgrim, to contend with dangerous enemies; and whereas each of Christian's enemies met him just once and was defeated once for all, man's greatest enemies, though often defeated, constantly reappear. Three of the greatest are ignorance, superstition and prejudice, and the progress of enlightenment is a perpetual struggle against these three. It is not exclusively an intellectual struggle, for the forces resisting enlightenment include moral and religious attitudes and social and political institutions. So reason is always potentially, and often actually, a revolutionary force. Because of this, again, there have been many who have suffered for their devotion to reason, and reason has its martyrology just as religious movements have. Included in the roll are not only men who have suffered for their work in the study of nature, such as Anaxagoras, Roger Bacon or Galileo, but many others who have brought reason to bear upon political, social, moral and religious conventions, such as Socrates,

Abelard, Bruno, Spinoza. The struggle goes on, and we in our time are summoned to take part in it. There is no ascertainable limit to what reason may one day achieve in making man the master of his physical environment and of his own life, social and individual.

THE PRECEPT OF RATIONALITY

This myth incorporates a value-judgment, and from that value-judgment follows a precept which we may call the precept of rationality. It may be formulated very simply: think everything through. Wherever reason is applicable, apply it and be guided by the result. Do not commit yourself to views which have not first been subjected to rational criticism. As Berkeley has it, 'It is to me a sufficient reason not to believe in the existence of anything, if I see no reason for believing it'.

Of course this is a counsel of perfection. Our human limitations are such that no one can carry it out everywhere and to the full. We have to be content to apply the principle as fully as we can in those matters which seem to us of the greatest importance, to be always ready to analyse further as opportunity arises, and for the rest to hold all our beliefs under the unspoken qualification that 'after all, we may be wrong'. If we do this, we can claim to be fulfilling the precept of rationality.

It will be seen that this principle leads to the holding of fewer firm opinions, and to more disbelief and suspense of judgment, than would occur without it. For that reason it can appear as an impoverishment; the intellectually untrained generally regard it so, and show signs of fear and hostility when it is enunciated. On the other hand it can be seen as a purgation, ridding the mind of much which may be interesting, but may also be misleading. Indeed this is one of the reasons which can be given for the acceptance of the precept of rationality in the first place. Here are we in a universe full of possibilities favourable and unfavourable, and we can only act according to the notions we form about this universe. It is safer to know the extent of our ignorance than to harbour conceptions which may be misconceptions. This, which is wisdom for every individual, becomes a stringent imperative among those who work together in the republic of science and learning. Not that there is not also a more idealistic motive behind the rationality precept. Reason, as the capacity for methodical and critical thought, is part of what is widely seen as an absolute value in life, as part of the distinction and the dignity of man.

This principle, that we should make the most of thought that we can, by thinking as far as we can through every question, is not itself a principle of thought, a logical principle. It is an ethical imperative. Of the two reasons for accepting it which were mentioned in the last paragraph, one is a prudential reason and falls within the sphere of that prudential calculation on which so much of the imperatives of our social life is based. The other belongs with that eudaemonistic ethic which emphasises the importance of being human and acting humanly. In recognising this precept we have entered the field of the ethics of thinking.

The idea of an ethic of thinking is not frequently discussed, at least not explicitly under that name, though certain virtues in the field of thought are so widely recognised that they are almost commonplace. Such for example are intellectual honesty and open-mindedness. But the rationality precept as I have formulated it goes far beyond these. It does not merely say that we should think honestly and fairly when we do think, but it claims in principle that everything in life which can be brought within the range of thought should be so brought. If the further step is taken of identifying thought with scientific method, the precept acquires an even sharper edge. A hundred years ago W. K. Clifford, in an article entitled 'The Ethics of Belief', stated the precept of rationality in a rigorous and uncompromising form, and used it for a trenchant criticism of the unethical character (as he believed it to be) of religious belief. Many others then and since have done the same.

THE CASE AGAINST GOD-BELIEF

The case against God-assertion is as clear as the case for it, and we cannot be surprised that many people find it convincing.

It is said that God-belief is an integrating and liberating factor in life, but actually it is found to be a restricting and corrupting influence. Thus we are told that it gives an absolute sanction and infinite worth to intelligent personality, so strengthening the respect which we in any case feel for personality, and encouraging all those things in human life which manifest and develop intelligence. But this can only be true at a very abstract level, where philosophical theologians may be at home but the ordinary man is not. The ordinary man, looking at God as supreme personality, sees him also as the creator of the world; and what sort of a personality does that make him? It makes him the author of a universe in which physical suffering and moral evil run riot. No, we learn nothing encouraging about personality from contemplating God; we only find ourselves faced by the suspicion that our human moral consciousness is less typical of the nature of the All-Agent than the theist pretends. Is this what he means by claiming that theism 'gives man a significant place in the universe'? Clearly it is not, and his claim falls to the ground.

But he also says that his belief opens up a whole world of possible relationships between man and God, relationships which can grow to a high degree of intimacy and which are an undeniable enrichment to life. Here again let us forget the abstract formula and think how these relationships actually work out. Let us remember how God's rule over us and our obedience to him are based on fear, kept alive by repeated threats which resound through the scriptures; so that his patronage of certain moral rules means only that we observe these rules from fear of him instead of because we see them to be right. Living thus by rules and motivated by fear, our attitude to other people is apt to be censorious and rule-ridden. But if it is said that we progress from this atmosphere of fear to one filial love and friendship, that in turn is only a kind of emotional dependence which robs us of the chance of growing up into fully responsible persons. God, whether as terrifying or as loving, is in either case an enemy to the humanity of man.

This conclusion is greatly strengthened if we take into account the organisations and institutions to which God-belief gives rise. Their record in history has been lamentable. We need not deny that religious organisations have often mediated spiritual benefit to many of their individual adherents. We need not hesitate to allow that their political and social influence has often been good and progressive. We could concede a large number of such instances and yet find in the end that the scale tips heavily the other way. Accumulation of corporate wealth by exploitation of the public, political intrigue, moral and intellectual censorship, discouragement of curiosity and critical questioning, encouragement of conservative acquiescent attitudes of mind which favour the ruling and possessing classes, acceptance and active encouragement of wars in the interests of ecclesiastical power—such is the record. The individual apologist for theism does not as a rule mean to defend these things, and the individual adherent of a religious group will often (though not always) dissociate himself from the behaviour of the organisation to which he belongs and will argue that such consequences do not follow from the principles which he professes. But it is of little use to disown the consequences in theory where history draws them out so powerfully in action.

So far the moral and social effects of God-belief. But is its intellectual quality much better? If one could legitimately separate the belief from the social and political consequences and consider it in itself, would it make a much better showing? Its terms are incurably ambiguous and it evades difficult questions by perpetually altering the meanings of words. Its arguments are without logical force. It is a systematic misuse of the apparatus of logical discourse to give an appearance of authenticity to what is really no more than an imaginative fantasy. To spend time on it is to waste time and energy, and to give it houseroom in the mind is to encourage bad thought-habits and to discourage what are the real virtues of rational thinking. It is therefore to mutilate one's humanity.

What do we mean by the virtues of rational thinking? Two things. In the first place certain qualities of the thought-process itself, which may for the present purpose be summed up as clarity and rigour. And in the second place certain qualities which belong rather to the thinker than to the thought, personal qualities which encourage and are encouraged by clear and rigorous thinking. One such quality is what we may call rationality, meaning by that a firm disposition always to think as clearly and rigorously as one's ability and one's circumstances will allow. Another is honesty, and another is courage. Around these qualities and some others which go with them is built up the modern thought-ethic.

The traditional theist would of course have agreed verbally that clarity and rigour, honesty and courage, were virtues which a thinker should possess. But he did not understand their meaning as we do today. Only since the modern thought-revolution can we realise what these virtues involve, and that realisation makes theism incompatible with the integrity of a rational person.

TWO RIVAL LIFE-PARADIGMS

In the last chapter we drew a picture on conventional theist lines of the development of human personality up to the point where it is crowned by God-belief. It was a picture of man living in a world where he is essentially at home, and finding his way to a more and more intimate involvement with it, and through it with God. Against that we have now to put the new rationalist paradigm of human growth. It is a picture of man living in a world which is indifferent to his values and ideals, and in the last resort even to his existence. His only hope of building up a worth-while life-pattern is through the acquisition of knowledge, and through knowledge, of power. Rational thinking is his only way to do that; and therefore the central value, around which any acceptable life-pattern must be built, is rationality. Aesthetic appreciation and artistic creation may add interest to life and contribute in some ways to psychological balance, but they must not be so indulged as to weaken the critical intelligence in its pursuit of objective reality. A system of *mores* is of course necessary to enable us to live and work together, but it should have no room for principles and practices, based on mere sentiment, which tend to weaken our potential as a rationally thinking race. We have no God to guide, guard and inspire us. Reason cannot entertain the proposition that he exists; and to indulge the fantasy of his existence is to weaken our critical consciousness, on which all our hopes must depend. In this critical consciouness we see not merely the necessary precondition of fruitful human development, but also the value which constitute our human dignity. To live self-delivered from ignorance and superstition and prejudice, self-dependent and spiritually free in a world where nothing and no one but ourselves appreciates what that means, that is what it means, that is what we resolve it shall mean, to be man.

A SOLUTION BY REASON?

Here then we have two paradigms for thought and life, two pictures of what it can mean to be man living in a world. Each is consistent in itself, and they are irreconcilable. Each constitutes a 'philosophy' in the old-fashioned sense of that word; but we can no longer think, as easily as our ancestors did, that the issue between one such 'philosophy' and another can be settled by rational argument. For neither of these two is composed exclusively of reality-statements, both include value-judgments and preferential attitudes, which are not rational as that word is generally understood. Is there then any rational way of deciding between them?

Some will say that of course there is, because one of the contenders is rationality itself and its rival is something outside reason. Obviously (they will say) the rationalistic paradigm is the one which every rational person must and will accept Such a reaction will be automatic on the part of many of our contemporaries, and there is no doubt that many philosophers will be among them. For it is generally agreed that a philosopher should be pre-eminently a man of reason, and it is easy to think that that involves committing himself to the rationalistic pattern of life and thought.

But though we may agree that the philosopher should be a man of reason, it is not evident that 'reason' in this precept is identical with the rationalisitc thought-pattern. For philosophy is not science. Being a man of reason, for a philosopher, should mean making a critical appraisal of all principles and commitments, including the commitment to rationalistic thought-patterns and the alleged necessity of that commitment for all thinkers in all fields. For what after all is a rational person? One, I suggest, who accepts what I have called the precept of rationality. But both the rival thought-patterns with which we are concerned accept it, at any rate verbally. Both lay great stress upon intelligence, or reason in the broad sense, as a central factor in what makes humanity human. Both urge us to cultivate our intelligence, to develop our rational capacities, to the full. Where they differ is in the interpretation of these words. What *are* our rational capacities, and what *is* it to develop them to the full?

On the one view, rationality means thinking on scientific lines, and no reality-assertions not reached along those lines can be legitimate. It is a clear and simple view, and if it is accepted, theism is ruled out.

On the other hand one could quote Aristotle's pregnant observation, that we should suit our methods and our expectations to what the subject-matter will allow, recognising that this will not be everywhere the same. Scientific method is right for science, but it does not follow that there are no other thought-processes by which other kinds of reality-assertions may legitimately be arrived at. One could contend that theological thinking is a thought-process of this kind, and that theological assertions are justified by the grounds on which they are made. One would have to add that it is important to remember what kind of thinking theology is, and not claim for it an authority comparable with that which belongs to science.

A philosopher can take either side in this dispute. It is possible to construct a philosophy of scientific empiricism which explicitly excludes all God-discourse, and to organise the world of human experience within that framework. And it is possible to construct a religious philosophy which includes the God-doctrine and makes it the centre of reference for everything else. Philosophies of both kinds still find authors and supporters. For myself, however, I should hesitate to put forward a philosophy of either type; for I should require more decisive reasons than I can actually find. All I can do is to state the issue and try to probe more deeply into what lies behind it.

To probe more deeply – but in search of what? In search of any possibility of resolving the issue. And the issue is between two rival paradigms for human thinking. We could not decide it by appeal to the precept of rationality, just because both sides in their own ways recognise the precept, and the conflict is reborn as a conflict over the meaning of 'reason' as a norm for thought. Can we resolve this in turn by some kind of appeal to reason? Is there a sense in which one interpretation of 'reason' can be more rational than another? Is there a reason behind reason, or some other principle behind reason, by reference to which the rival interpretations could be judged?

A SOLUTION BY GOING BEHIND REASON

Let us remember that we are not now operating in the field of logic. 'Reason' as we are now discussing it is normative principle, and the precept of rationality is an ethical imperative. The deeper principle which we are seeking, whether we think fit to call it also 'reason' or not, will be found in that region from which all norms proceed; it will be related to the will as we have used that word in speaking of a will to live, or to live thus and thus. And therefore it would seem that we cannot establish it as a valid principle by logical argument, but that it is here as it is generally with value-judgments and attitudes, that we cannot go beyond persuasive exposition.

We are looking, then, for a basic attitude, a really deep-seated value-creating principle, to which we could appeal for a decision. The appeal would consist in asking which of our two rival standpoints gives fuller and truer expression to the basic attitude.

That would provide a reason, not a reason of logic but of the kind appropriate in the sphere of value-discourse, for preferring one standpoint to the other. Is there such a basic principle?

One could invoke (a) the will to live, which is the most basic principle of all. But it is not specific enough. What else? (b) All human cultural activities are expressions of the will to live thus and thus. Is there something for us here? Can we find something to our purpose implicit in that phrase 'thus and thus'? Not if the difference between one manner of living and another is merely qualitative; the preference in such a case must be purely personal. But what if it is intensive? We should then have the principle of (c) fullness of life to work with. And this sounds promising, because both our rival standpoints are sometimes defended by appeal to it. Cannot we, as a third party, draw our own conclusion as to which of them better exemplifies it?

Both standpoints promise fullness of life; and that shows the weakness of the principle, for they could not appeal to it and remain opposed as they are, were it not that the fullness of life means different things to the two of them. The God-believer points to the diversity in unity of the different human activities, invigorated severally and collectively by their common reference to God as supreme Being and Value; to the variety and deep significance of personal relationships between human beings, and between each human being and his God; and to the window on infinity opened up by our connection with the Absolute. In all this he sees a richly endowed human personality set in a richly diversified physical and social world, interacting with his surroundings and progressively enriched and deepened by these interactions. That (he says) is fullness of life; that is what flows from the acknowledgment of God. But the scientific rationalist points to the inhibiting and impoverishing effects of ignorance, superstition and prejudice, and to the liberation of human energies by the progressive overcoming of these evils; to the increasing freedom from fear brought about by knowledge and power even in a dangerous universe; and to man growing to self-conscious maturity as master of his world and of himself. In all this he sees the epic struggle, successful though against odds, of a humanity enriched and deepened by the perpetual challenge under which it lives. And that (to him) is fullness of life; that is what flows from the surrender of metaphysical fantasies and the acceptance of facts as they are.

We have here two assessments of the human situation, two views of what it is to be a human being living in a world. Or rather, two views of what *should be* the meaning of human existence, and therefore of what view of our situation in the universe *should* be or *shall* taken. They are two existentialisms, the well-known pair or rivals, existentialism with God and existentialism without God. And between them there seems to be no argument, only a competition in dogmatic assertion and rejection. Each is watertight against taking seriously what the other regards as central. And we, the onlooking philosophers, who stand far enough aloof to be able to state both sides of the dispute, can do nothing to reconcile them. One can try to clear up misconceptions, which are always rife when metaphysical issues are at stake; but neither side has an unlimited receptivity for such clarifications. In any case what keeps them apart is not disagreement about terms, but a different preference as between rival joys and rival virtues. Each side regards the virtues of the other side as inferior virtues, and its joys as joys unworthily purchased and hollow. And because the conflict is never resolved, neither case can ever be stated finally and once for all. For the landscape of the battlefield changes in the course of history, and each claimant must constantly justify itself afresh. It is a perpetual dialectic not of arguments, but of standpoints, and a dialectic which finds no synthesis.

15 Choice, No Choice and Self-Choice

Metaphysical belief or unbelief depends on an act of preference, an acceptance of one view in preference to another, and for this preference no logical justification can be given. Are we then to say that belief or unbelief is a matter of choice? Yes, perhaps, though only in a qualified sense. If it is a choice, there is much to be said about the kind of choice that it is.

BELIEF AS RESPONSIBLE ACT

People who adopt beliefs divergent from those of groups to which they belong are sometimes reproached for it. They are told that they have adopted these views wantonly, irresponsibly, for unworthy reasons. To this the victim replies that he is not professing this belief because he wants to; that belief is involuntary and depends on evidence; and that the evidence constrains him to this conclusion.

As an assertion of one's own integrity this sounds fine. But experience and reflection show that belief is not, absolutely and without qualification, involuntary. We are not helpless in the grip of evidence. For to begin with, it rests with us how closely we attend to the evidence, how critical we are of first impressions, and how wide we fling the net of enquiry. Then, too, it is sometimes a question how much weight should be given to one consideration, in itself or in comparison with other considerations; and this giving weight to considerations is something that the thinker himself does. In these ways an element of voluntariness enters into our beliefs in all those matters which are not determinable by strict logic, but depend on the balancing of one point against another. And so those who blame the misbeliever are not being wholly unreasonable. They may be wrong in their diagnosis of his motives in believing as he does, but they are not wrong in their underlying assumption that he has motives as well as reasons, that his belief is a morally responsible act.

HAVING TO CHOOSE FOR ONESELF

Many people, while knowing as a fact that there are believers in God and non-believers, and that the believers do not all believe exactly the same thing, do not feel called upon to make a personal decision in the matter. At least, the only decision which they are ever conscious of being called to make is the decision to take their beliefs seriously. One of the many types of experience to which the name 'conversion' is given is this, when someone who has been habitually professing certain beliefs but drifting through life regardless of their implications, wakes up to these implications and resolves to follow them out in practice. One can do this without feeling any need to call in question the substance of one's beliefs or to consider replacing them by others. If they are what one has grown up to believe, and what all or most people in one's environment believe, no issue arises. One's beliefs are determined by cultural influences, and no question of personal decision enters in.

The historian, taking a broad view of men's religious beliefs, is bound to see this as the typical case. He sees whole societies going on from century to century holding the same religious views with minimal modifications, obviously because these views are handed down by cultural transmission and there is no effective counter-influence. Whatever may be the deep roots of religious belief in general, the religion of a particular society at a particular time is a historical product. The history of religion is part of the history of human society as a whole, and of the various cultural moulds in which it crystallises itself. The social sciences give depth and colour to the historian's picture, the sociology of religion tracing variations of belief and practice in so far as they correlate with social class, occupation, political influences, education and so on, and the psychology of religion showing the impact of religious influences upon the individual with all his personal peculiarities. In sum, it appears that a man's religious belief is a function of the society into which he is born, his place within that society and his personal character and circumstances. As a general rule he takes the shape which these influences give to him, without feeling the need to make any significant choice in the matter.

Of course this socio-historical determinism of beliefs has its own interest for the philosopher, but more interesting to him is the case where social and psychological influences conspire to thrust upon the individual a degree of conscious and deliberate determination where a man is conscious of an issue concerning the substance of his belief, an issue which he has to determine for himself. This can be the case for large numbers at a time when one culture clashes with another, when a man cannot merely adhere to what he has been taught, but must make up his own mind where he stands. This can happen when the domain of one religious tradition is invaded by influences carrying another religion with them; but it is happening in a new form today as the domains of all the religious traditions are invaded by the new science-inspired culture which doubts or denies any kind of God-belief whatsoever. Those in whom there is something which responds to the new and challenging influence are compelled to decide between what education has so far made them and what the new influence invites them to become. They have to find themselves, to find that commitment which promises to realise their best potentialities, and in that sense to become their true selves.

A decision like this is what Kierkegaard and his successors have taught us to call an existential choice.

EXISTENTIAL CHOICE

Making choices is of the very substance of our lives. We are continually being presented with alternative possibilities of thought or of action, and accepting one possibility in preference to another. Most of the time nothing of deep significance is involved; the alternatives all fall within the range of our regular habits of thought and action, and represent merely different ways of securing our every-day ends such as food and clothing and shelter and comfort and pleasure of various kinds. Even on the relatively rare occasions when a serious moral problem arises, we do not set to work to alter our accepted moral principles, but merely to work out the best way of applying them in complex circumstances. The choice is made, the occasion passes, and we go on living as the same persons that we were before.

But there are some choices, existential choices, after making which one is never quite the same person again. Such is the adoption of a religious (or in some instances a political) allegiance, of a vocation, of a commitment to some cause, of a celibate life or of a marriage partner, and the like. These are not instances of deciding what to do in the present moment, but of deciding what kind of life to live, what kind of person to be, for an indefinite future. So one may be said to be choosing oneself, one's future self that is to say. And one does it with one's eyes open. Existential choice is self-choice not only in the merely consequential sense that it will have results which will affect me deeply, but in the sense that I see in principle (not of course in detail) what my future self is to be, and consciously resolve to be that kind of self, to live that kind of life, to have that kind of consciousness. There is in it a thrill of conscious self-becoming.

Kierkegaard was one who had experience of such choices in his own life, and made them with full awareness of what he was doing. And in his philosophical writings he gave us a doctrine of the spiritual way in terms of a process involving existential choices at decisive points. He describes four possible life-attitudes (aesthetic, ethical, religious and Christian), and they form a progression by which one may rise to the height of maturity.

I am not here concerned to trace any such progression. The only existential choice with which I am concerned is the choice between the God-accepting and the God-refusing world-perspectives as described above. The decision may of course go either way. My desire is to probe a little further into what happens when the decision is made, whichever way it goes.

THE CHALLENGE OF THE AUTHENTIC SELF

We speak of choice, and in the moment of decision we feel that we are making a choice. And yet there is a sense in which we may also feel that after all we really have no choice. One view or the other imposes itself; or something imposes it upon us, not as an external force doing us violence, but somehow as from within. It is not merely a seeing of the truth; it is coming to one's true self.

Here is a paradox. Existential choice is a self-making choice, we said. But now this choice, which *makes* the self what it is to be henceforward, seems in a deeper sense to *express* the self as it already is. The new truth presenting itself for acceptance seems to be a projection from the deep-seated attitudes and drives of the self. Deliberation, ostensibly an examination of the new truth which offers itself, seems to be in a deeper sense a process of self-search and self-discovery. And so the decision 'I choose this' really means 'in this I recognise my true self'.

How is it possible that there should be a choice which is no choice? Or that in becoming what we are not yet we should be becoming what we already are?

If in choosing we advance to our true self, that must mean that our starting-point, our self as it is before the choice, is not our true self. And how can that be? Because the self is not an object of a kind which is from the outset all that it is to be, but a living thing which is always growing into what it is to be. At birth it is phenomenally almost a *tabula rasa*, though no doubt it has concealed potentialities which time and experience must actualise. The first influences to shape it are influences from without, from physical environment and family and society. Only later does the self, becoming self-conscious, acquire the power of self-shaping, and then, as often as not, it is found that the beliefs and habits with which it has grown up do not properly express its deeper attitudes and tendencies as it progressively discovers them. So there arises a need to change the phenomenal self, perhaps quite radically, to give the deeper potential self a chance to find expression and satisfaction. It is here that the real choice lies in an existential decision: which of two competing systems of beliefs and attitudes will the more fully liberate the deeper self. I choose this, I identify myself with this and throw myself open to be shaped by it, because only this can I become in act and fact what in my deepest being I already am.

This is what the existentialist writers mean by their talk of authentic and inauthentic existence. Many people, not of the existentialist school, nevertheless see the point and talk of the all-importance of what they call integrity.

Some people, on finding their deep self, find that they have to cast off a great deal of what society has brought them up to be and to do. Their phenomenal self belies their true self and cannot be readjusted, but only stripped off. But this does not happen to all, and there is no necessity in principle that it should. It is not impossible that a person should grow up in habits and traditions which, for him, give free scope for the unfolding of his deep self. In Christian language, not all are called to the more spectacular forms of self-discipline and renunciation; one can quite well have a true vocation to serve God in the social position to which one has grown up. Kierkegaard remarks that the 'knight of faith' may look just like a city clerk, may in fact be one; only he is not *merely* a city clerk, there is something deep down in him which the outward eye does not see. Any man's humanity is inauthentic is so far as he has not seen into the depths of himself and found a form of phenomenal life which expresses what he finds there. One may well ask, has anyone ever fully met this requirement? Very likely no one; but people do differ in the degree to which they approach it, and the differences are enormous, and enormously important.

AN UNANSWERABLE QUESTION

Here may arise yet again the question whether we can go behind the two rival thought-paradigms, not this time in the sense of bringing the parties to a common mind, but of seeing for ourselves that one of them is not probing deeply enough into the nature of man. It is tempting to assume that human nature is fundamentally homogeneous that differences are phenomenal but there is unity in the depths, and that therefore if the two parties continue to differ as they do, one of them is misreading the depths. The parties themselves in fact both take this line, each asserting that its own view is ultimately right and that the other side is failing to look deep enough. The theist party say that, since we are all God's creatures and bearers of his image, on our deepest levels we are all geared to God. To find one's deepest self is to find God, and to find God is to find one's deepest self. The other party say that God is indeed a projection of something in our own selves, but not in our deepest selves. The deepest self is the reason-loving and critical self, which, when it finds full expression must see through the God-illusion.

To us, I believe, both assertions are dogmatic and essentially matters of faith. For ourselves, we can register the empirical diversity of human minds and personalities, and of the social and historical influences which bear upon them, and of the degrees of authenticity which they severally achieve. Our own philosophical integrity requires us to refrain from asserting more than we can ascertain.

16 Analytical Philosophy and the Believer

Let us now sum up our results:

(1) The foundation of theism is not a speculative guess or inference or theory, but an imaginative vision of existence which can be of deep significance for life.

(2) It cannot be verified by common sense or by science or by metaphysics.

(3) There is a gamut of religious experience which strengthens the impression that in our approaches to 'God' we are in touch with something real, but it does not prove it. And one aspect of experience is that the meanings of our images and concepts are constantly changing in our hands.

(4) What determines belief is an existential acceptance. Man builds a world around himself and builds himself in relation to that world. 'God' is a way of obtaining maximum unity in the world and maximum meaningfulness in our life. But the acceptance of God is not an ascertainment of existing fact, but a kind of 'faith'.

(5) There is a rival 'faith' which presents a world and a life without 'God'.

(6) No decision can be made between the rival faiths on rational grounds. Adherence to either, in so far as it is not mere habit, is a kind of choice. One chooses that belief which allows expression to one's authentic self.

(7) It is tempting to suppose that, if we could all analyse ourselves to the deepest level, we should find the authentic self to be the same in us all, and therefore converge upon a common faith. But it has never yet been found possible to make such an analysis and reach such a convergence.

The reader who has endured so far may naturally ask whether

this indecisive conclusion is the end of the matter. And as far as philosophy is concerned I think it is. No doubt there are philosophers who will put forward a definite result, some of them accepting the case for a theist metaphysic and others accepting the case against it. To me both ways appear to deviate from the royal road of philosophy. Each is an existential choice; and in my view, while it is philosophy's business to show what existential choices are and why one cannot live without making them, it is not philosophy's business to make them. When the philosopher comes out as a theist or as a non-theistic humanist, life is prevailing over thought. And it is proper that life should have the last word, only not in philosophy, which is not actual life but critical reflection upon life. Because this book is an essay in philosophy, it cannot go beyond the sceptical conclusion to which its reflection leads.

But the reader may retort that the author of the book is a living man. He may ask what kind of a living man the author is. Does he identify himself with the negative result of his argument, and so withdraw from life? Or does he choose one of the rival faiths, and if so, which one? And what place does he find, in a life committed to one faith, for an activity of philosophical reflection which seeks so anxiously to do justice to both, and ends by casting doubt upon both?

I do not think I am obliged to answer these questions. On the other hand I see no reason to refuse. Let it be said, then, that I am a theist of the standard type, a practising adherent of one of the Christian Churches and a student of the thought and life of them all. The reader who remembers Chapters 9 and 11 of this book will of course not overestimate the amount which these statements entitle him to conclude about my actual beliefs. He will not be wrong in thinking that I recite the Creed and frequent the Eucharist, but he cannot know how far I have gone along the road of demythologisation and reinterpretation which is described in those chapters. To tell him that would require nothing less than another book.

Still he may ask how the philosopher and the believer in me manage to coexist. What does the sceptical philosopher in me think of the believer? And what does the believer make of the philosopher's activites? But the answer to the first of these questions has been given; it is the content of this book. That leaves the second question outstanding. I have given a philosophical interpretation and assessment of theism. Can I now give a theist interpretation and assessment of this kind of philosophy?

The question is no novelty to me. If I had failed to think of it myself, the world would not have let me overlook it. Both among religious believers and outside their ranks it is widely held that sincere belief is incompatible with any ultimate scepticism. The believer must be sure of his God, and that (so it is thought) requires that he should have what he at least considers to be objective reasons for his belief. The faithful, at least in the Christian Church, are instructed that the entertaining of doubts is sinful. Yet here am I pursuing a course which opens up one doubt after another, and pushing it to the point where, philosophically speaking at any rate, doubt has the last word. And it is a peculiarly wicked kind of doubt, namely relativism, which is taken to mean that even if we do arrive at any beliefs about God, they will include no element of reality-recognition, but will simply be projections of our own shifting fancies. No wonder, where such views are held, that even honest and intelligent men refuse to believe that an honest use of intelligence can lead to such conclusions as those of this book.

For myself, having been brought to these conclusions, I have no wish to evade them. That this is where philosophy leads I have found to be a fact, and the fact must be interpreted. How does a Christian interpret the fact that philosophy, pursued as best he can pursue it, brings him to a sceptical or relativist position?

I say that the situation is not surprising if man is what experience shows him to be, and what Christianity confesses him to be. His liability to fundamental doubt springs directly from his dependence on discursive reason. We may fairly presume that the lower animals do not spend time doubting what their senses present to them, or seeking significances and implications beyond what is manifest to eye and snout. They are sometimes perplexed when confronted with something unfamiliar, but they look again, and sniff again, until their instincts can deliver a verdict. They do not frame intellectual puzzles and plunge into metaphysics. On the other hand it is equally clear that (to speak with the Christians for the occasion) the angels with their purely intuitive intelligence do not doubt the vision of God which is their life and their felicity. We may say the same of the blessed souls in heaven; for although they are human, and *ratio* is a capacity inherent in human nature, their situation must greatly limit its use, if not supersede it altogether. The compelling splendour of the beatific vision must leave ratiocination far behind. Thus the beasts do not share our doubts because they are below the level at which rational reflection raises questions, while the angels and the blessed do not share them because they are above that level. It is we in this present life, *in via* as the Christians say, who are wide open to all these perplexities. Relativity is part of our condition as human beings in this present world.

Looking around us at the world in which we live, we find the structure of the not-self mediated to us through the lenses of our sensibility, and its obstinate reality everywhere confronting us. In speaking of this not-self we use object-language, which is the common tradition of our race, and so the massive edifice of common sense is built up and maintained, and scientific discovery increasingly added to that. But then comes critical reflection of the kind which leads to philosophy, and it brings with it uncertainty and obscurity. For although the object is no creation of ours, but a reality which compels our attention, still we cannot either perceive or conceive it except in terms which bear the impress of our own nature upon them. We can ask, verbally, what the object may be in itself, but in the long run we can attach no meaning to this phrase. And though the assumptions, conjectures and theories by which our world-picture is filled out are undoubtedly verified to some extent by experience, yet continuing reflection shows that we verify less than we often think we do.

Looking towards God, we see in intuitive vision the lineaments of the All-Agent; and in the persistence or perpetual recurrence of the vision, as well as in various other aspects of experience, we seem to ourselves to feel the continuing pressure of a reality. We speak of this reality in the rich, suggestive but incurably ambiguous God-language of the various theist traditions. But then comes critical reflection and brings with it uncertainty and obscurity. For even if God is no invention of ours, but a reality which claims our attention, still we cannot discern his presence, or imagine or conceive him, except in ways which translate his reality into terms of our experience. We can only conceive his nature on the analogy of our own, though it needs little reflection to make us aware that the analogy is inexact; and the deeper natural theology goes into the question, the more the mysteriousness of God's being overshadows what we thought was our knowledge of him. And though the experiences which seem to illustrate and confirm our belief in him are likely to continue and multiply as we move along the spiritual way, yet, if we keep our critical wits about us, it becomes increasingly hard to say what exactly they do illustrate and confirm.

If such is our situation, clear consequences follow. The

philosopher-believer or believer-philosopher must harbour no dream of escaping from the sceptical predicament. He must learn to integrate it into his belief, so that the God whom he acknowledges is a God who has himself placed us in this situation, and whom we best honour by accepting the fact. There is in fact scriptural predicament for the recognition that the true God is one who hides himself and is girt about with darkness and mystery, but hitherto the principle has not generally been interpreted in the way here suggested. The time has now come when it must be so interpreted.

I have often thought that one way to understand the position of the philosopher-believer in our times would be to consider the figure of an earlier philosopher-believer, St Anselm, and see how our present situation differs from his. I shall bring this discussion to a close by doing that.

Few perhaps of those who study the ontological argument as a philosopheme go on to study its author as a man. Few perhaps of those who consult chapters 2–4 of the *Proslogion* go on to see what can be learned from the literary character of the book as a whole. The ontological argument is of course a purely intellectual exercise, like much else that is in the book; but the book as a whole is something of a different kind. As its title proclaims, it is couched in the form of a meditation wherein the author addresses alternately his own soul and God. That means that it is a religious exercise; and so we are led to ask what a piece of pure philosophy is doing in such an exercise, and what its presence there can tell us about Anselm's personality and outlook.

The answer to the first of these questions is clear enough. Anselm is rooted in a tradition which goes back to Philo and St Paul and the early Fathers, according to which there can be no understanding, in matters relating to God, unless there is first of all faith. The contention is not that one should believe instead of understanding. On the contrary, it is made clear that what is at first believed should, as and when and in so far as may be possible, be raised to the level of understanding. But faith must come first, because it is only from within the life of faith that one can learn the meaning of the terms used, and so see what is really at issue.

It is clear that this is how Anselm's mind works. His philosophical argument turns on the definition of 'God' as 'the greatest thinkable'. Whence does he get this concept? According to his own account, not from free metaphysical speculation, but from the faith of the Church. Actually 'the greatest thinkable' was never an official formula of Church teaching. What is really happening is that Anselm shares the God-vision with all his fellow-Christians, and 'the greatest thinkable' is his own conceptualisation of it in terms of the metaphysical tradition in which he has been trained. It is the only concept in that idiom which seems to him adequately to represent the object of the vision. So he analyses it and believes himself to discover in it an inherent logical certitude of being the concept of something real. The modern Anselm, if anyone exists who can be so described, will not be deceived by the ontological argument, but he will be like the original Anselm in that he will begin from the God-vision, and his argument, however it develops, will be essentially an analysis and assessment of that.

One most instructive feature of Anselm's work is his treatment of the concept of the Fool, the *insipiens* who says in his heart *non est Deus*. There cannot have been many professed atheists in Anselm's circle, but he knows from Scripture that they exist, and their existence is a challenge to his whole argument. For he has proved to his own satisfaction not only that God certainly exists, but that his non-existence is inconceivable; how then can anyone assert it? How is the Fool possible? Anselm replies with a piece of linguistic analysis. He deduces the possibility of denying the existence of God from the possibility of misconceiving what the word 'God' means. If one knows that it means the greatest thinkable, then the non-existence of God is unthinkable. But if one understands the word 'God' in any other sense than that, it becomes possible to conceive and to assert his non-existence.

Today the worker in natural theology is not necessarily a Christian, not necessarily a God-believer at all; and if he is, his position will be very different from Anselm's. Yet he will have advantages if he is like Anselm in speaking from within the believing community (though that community will be immensely wider and more diversified for him than it was for Anselm). He will analyse the God-vision and explicate the grounds and motives of assent, as I have done in this book. But whereas the older Anselm's analysis seemed to reveal the logical strength of the believer's position, the modern Anselm's analysis will reveal its logical weakness and its dependence on an existential acceptance to produce assent. In a word, the modern Anselm will find that the Fool is inside his own mind, an ineradicable aspect of his own personality.

The Fool has to be taken much more seriously today than in the twelfth century. Although it is true that differences of linguistic convention play an important part in the controversy, he cannot be simply dismissed as the victim of a semantic mistake. There is immensely more to him than that. He represents one of the most creative and challenging cultural and spiritual forces of our time. To take him seriously is an act of respect both for him as a man and the bearer of a concept of authentic humanity, and for God who, if indeed he exists, apparently does not will to be ascertained, but only to be divined, by human beings.

In fact, if the modern natural theologian stands to gain by being some kind of a believer, he must also be able and willing to stand apart from his belief, to watch himself and others believing and to describe what he sees from a standpoint which is itself outside belief. He must also insert himself into the rival standpoint and describe that as fairly and adequately as he can. He must go as far as he can in search of a basis on which the conflict might be rationally resolved. If I am right, however, he will find that philosophy does not prove either view, but brings us to the point where the *man* decides. But the man's own integrity requires that, in deciding, he should not disown the philosopher.

Index

Abelard, 160
Anaxagoras, 159
Anselm, St, 64, 72, 73, 74, 179, 180
Aquinas, St Thomas, 61, 64, 87, 112, 128
Aristotle, 61, 65, 66, 165
Augustine, St, 73, 122
Ayer, A. J., 19, 21, 22

Bacon, Roger, 159
Berkeley, G., 49, 91, 160
Bonaventura, 87
Bradley, F. H., 70, 95, 96
Braithwaite, R. B., 41, 142
Bruno, 160
Buddhism, 57, 88, 122, 132, 141
Bunyan, J., 159

Christianity, 4, 8, 31, 32, 42, 58, 105, 129, 157, 177
Clifford, W. K., 161

De Sales, St Francis, 105
Descartes, R., 64, 72
Duns Scotus, 64, 87, 112

Existentialism, 168

Farrer, A. M., 48
Flew, A. G. N., 19, 24, 28, 33

Galileo, 159
Gifford, Lord, 9
Gregory Nazianzen, St, 123
Gregory of Nyssa, St, 123

Hegel, G. W. F., 70, 73
Hinduism, 8, 55, 132
Hume, D., 22

Islam, 4, 8, 42, 105, 132

Jefferies, R., 130
John of the Cross, St, 132
Judaism, 4, 8, 42, 58
Jung, C. G., 40, 142

Kant, I., 60, 77, 87, 148
Kierkegaard, S., 171, 172, 173
Krishna, 55

Leibniz, G., 115
Lull, R., 27n

Muhammed, 105

Nietzsche, F. W., 155, 156

Otto, R., 58, 59, 121, 122

Paul, St, 179
Philo, 179
Plato, 70, 73, 88, 95
Platonism, 76, 78, 88, 153
Plotinus, 95

Reformation, 157
Renaissance, 10
Ruysbroeck, 105

Sayers, Dorothy, 39
Smart, J. J. C., 89n
Socrates, 159
Spinoza, B., 38, 40, 115, 130, 160
Stoicism, 9, 78, 153

Webb, C. C. J., 74
Wesley, Charles, 107
Whitehead, A. N., 108